AMERICA'S
FOOTBALL
FACTORY

WAYNE ST  oy Mike Ditka

AMERICA'S

Western Pennsylvania's

FOOTBALL

Cradle of Quarterbacks from

FACTORY

Johnny Unitas to Joe Montana

SECOND EDITION

Black Squirrel Books®
Kent, Ohio

ISBN 978-1-60635-351-6
Manufactured in the United States of America

Black Squirrel Books®
Frisky, industrious black squirrels are a familiar sight on the Kent State University campus and
the inspiration for Black Squirrel Books®, a trade imprint of The Kent State University Press.
www.KentStateUniversityPress.com

Cataloging information for this title is available at the Library of Congress.

22 21 20 19 18   5 4 3 2 1

To the Stewart family: My wife Nancy, our sons Sean and Scott, daughters-in-law Rachel and Katie, and our grandson Nathan. Also, to my parents: O. J. Stewart, who taught me to love words, and Margaret (Jones) Stewart, who taught me the joy of reading.

CONTENTS

FOREWORD

I GREW UP in Western Pennsylvania in the town of Aliquippa, which produced almost as many football players as it did steel. I believe Aliquippa High School has sent 11 players to the NFL. I was one of those men, playing my college football for the Pitt Panthers before moving on to the NFL, playing there for the Chicago Bears, the Philadelphia Eagles, and the Dallas Cowboys from 1961 to 1972.

A few other stars out of Aliquippa include two All-Pros, Ty Law and Darrelle Revis, and you can toss in Sean Gilbert, who was on a Pro Bowl team once. Having one kid make it to the NFL out of a small town is a noteworthy accomplishment. To produce multiple NFL players is to defy incredibly long odds—but, then again, determined Western Pennsylvanians have a long history of doing just that.

I have always had a warm spot in my heart for Western Pennsylvania and the people of that area, from towns such as Donora, which produced men I admire greatly in Stan Musial and Deacon Dan Towler, to Monessen, which also sent more than 10 players to the NFL, and to places such as Beaver Falls, home of nine pro players, including Joe Namath, Jim Mutscheller, and Joe Walton.

The area around Pittsburgh was packed with people who wanted to better themselves and who were very competitive. For example, I always strived to show that I was as good as anyone. Our rugged blue-collar attitude and strong work ethic helped carry us to success.

I've always believed that you can be anything that you want to be if you work hard for it. Western Pennsylvanian athletes were given the chance to take their skills, diligently work on them, and then carve out a good career for themselves. My part of the country—and for that matter, our entire nation—has always been a great land of opportunity.

As I said, Western Pennsylvania has churned out many great athletes in general, but somehow, again, *against all odds*, the area was able to manufacture an unbelievably high percentage of standout quarterbacks and export them to the highest levels of football.

A kid doesn't start playing football thinking that he'll eventually make it to the Hall of Fame—they start because they love the game. Still, six kids from Western Pennsylvania were able to turn their love of the game into outstanding Hall of Fame careers.

You can't get much better than the primary six men featured in this book: the ageless, highly competitive George Blanda; Johnny Unitas, the man I consider to have started something big by perfecting the forward pass as a vital, frequent weapon; Joe Namath, who was as tough as nails; Joe Montana, an unbelievable quarterback I had to coach against; Dan Marino, who, like me, went to Pitt and set records; and Jim Kelly, who turned the Buffalo Bills into a winner. What a group!

MIKE DITKA, Hall of Fame tight end

ACKNOWLEDGMENTS

THANKS GO OUT to the following people, listed in no particular order: Betsy McGurgan, Steve Higgins, and Ken Thomas of Beaver Falls, for their help regarding Joe Namath. Chad Unitas, Shirley (Unitas) Green, Paige Unitas, Leonard Unitas, Sandy Unitas, Joe Unitas, Fred Cox, Chuck Crummie, Carl Crawley, Joe Emanuele, Rudy Andabaker, Rich Erdelyi, Steve Russell, Joe Ravasio, Paul Zolak, Scott Zolak, Mike Ditka, Mike Lucci, Raymond Berry, Rick Volk, Tom Matte, Ken MacAfee, Lenny Moore, Gino Marchetti, Ulice Payne, Jim Houston, Sam Havrilak, Andy Nelson, John Ziemann, Mike Gallagher, Rick Slager, Kris Haines, Tom Caudill, Stanley Fabin, Vagas Ferguson, Bernie Galiffa, Bimbo Cecconi, Terry Henry, Speer Ruey, Tim Stokes, David Sarkus, Chuck Smith, and to all the people who gave up their time and shared their memories and expertise when they agreed to be interviewed for this book.

THE CRADLE
OF QUARTERBACKS

WESTERN PENNSYLVANIA IS a slice of the country that is peppered with geographic names of American Indian origins. Towns that boast of producing star players such as Joe Montana also proudly bear names such as that of his hometown, Monongahela. It is also a part of the country teeming with football talent dating back to . . . well, not quite as far back as the days when Native Americans alone populated the country, but certainly back to the earliest days of the sport's existence.

In fact, some of the game's oldest roots are firmly planted in Pennsylvania soil. The first professional football game ever played was between the Pittsburgh Athletic Club and the Allegheny Athletic Association. On November 12, 1892, the victorious Allegheny team's illegal action of paying one of its players—a William Heffelfinger—made their game that day, the first professional football contest. Furthermore, the Latrobe Athletic Association, a Pennsylvania squad that existed from 1895 to 1909, is considered to be the first football team to play a complete season (1897) employing a full roster of professional players. Actually, the Allegheny Athletic Association had already been the first organization to field a complete roster of pros, but did so in its abbreviated 1896 season.

Then there was Grant Dibert, who signed the first known professional contract, joining the Pittsburgh Athletic Club in 1893; and John Brallier, who became the first player to openly play pro football when he was paid the princely sum of $10 in 1895 by the Latrobe YMCA team.

In addition, although it took more than a few decades to make the discovery, the Keystone State, *especially* the western part of that state, became the greatest area in the nation for producing quarterbacks. For that matter, it was also a fantastic area for the mass production of football stars, period—regardless of position played. Just ask fans of Tony Dorsett, Mike Ditka, Ty Law, Jim Covert, Bill Fralic, Curtis Martin, or Dan Towler,

Quick aside: Mike Gallagher, a sportscaster who went to the same Pittsburgh high school as Dan Marino, was, due to his friendship with Marino, invited to take part in a "Quarterback Challenge," sponsored by Jim Kelly for charity. Gallagher recalled:

> There'd be a hole just big enough to fit a football through it, and all the quarterbacks and celebrities would line up and throw a ball 30, 40 yards. If someone got it through the hole, their charity would get one million dollars.
>
> They picked one or two local media guys, so Danny makes the comment to Kelly, "I want Gallagher to throw—if he doesn't throw, I don't throw." I get up for my turn and threw a nice pass, a good, tight spiral. As it bounces off the target, Earl Morrall turns to Danny, "Hey, Marino, your reporter friend here has got an arm." Marino turns and says, "Of course he does; he's from Pittsburgh. Everybody from Pittsburgh can throw a football."

Well, not everybody, but it is staggering how many great arms came out of that area. Some experts go so far as to say the area is the most productive of any geographic area for turning out athletes, regardless of the position they play. The introductory commentary from a video entitled *The Greatest Moments in Western Pennsylvania Sports History* noted: "The families of a proud Pittsburgh and her surrounding communities have forged a hard-working tradition all their own. The offspring of this unwavering discipline and proud heritage was a breed of athlete that would soar above all others."

As far as football goes, it seems apparent that, if being endowed with the skills necessary to become a stellar quarterback is a from-the-cradle, God-given gift, then He must have favored those born in the Pittsburgh area, as He generously blessed them with a preponderance of talent.

It seems almost indisputable that Western Pennsylvania reigns as the greatest cradle of quarterbacks ever. Consider what the Rankopedia website listed as that area's top 10, dominated by men from the general Pittsburgh vicinity, with their countdown building up to their pick as the greatest of them all:

10. Marc Bulger (Pittsburgh) was a two-time All-Pro who threw for more than 22,000 yards in the NFL.
9. Gus Frerotte (Ford City) through 2016 is still in the top 100 for total yards passing in the NFL.

8. Jeff Hostetler (Hollsopple), along with Joe Montana, is one of only two quarterbacks to go from being a third-round draft player to starting and winning the Super Bowl.

7. George Blanda (Youngwood)—a chapter is devoted to him later in the book.

6. Johnny Lujack (Connellsville) won the 1947 Heisman Trophy; as a sophomore, he played halfback at times and also kicked and played defensive back as well. He led the NFL in touchdowns thrown, yards passing, attempts, and completions in his second year in the league and threw for a record 468 yards in one contest.

5. Jim Kelly (East Brady)—a chapter is devoted to him later in the book.

4. Joe Namath (Beaver Falls)—a chapter is devoted to him later in the book.

3. Dan Marino (Pittsburgh)—a chapter is devoted to him later in the book. Also from Marino's alma mater, Central Catholic High School, are Tino Sunseri, who called signals for the University of Pittsburgh, and Perry Hills, a University of Maryland quarterback.

2. Johnny Unitas (Pittsburgh)—a chapter is devoted to him later in the book.

1. Joe Montana (Monongahela)—a chapter is devoted to him later in the book.

Most geographic areas of the country would take, say, Jim Kelly and gladly claim him as their best; yet as great as he was, he could finish no higher on the list than fifth. Not only that, but when Johnny Unitas, who once held virtually every important quarterback record on the books, can muster only a second-place finish in such a poll, the area in which he grew up truly has a proliferation of talent.

Rankopedia's expanded list of the area's top 25 added 15 other first-rate quarterbacks from Western Pennsylvania:

25. Wally Foster (Oakmont)

24. Dan Darragh (Pittsburgh)

23. Arnold Galiffa (Donora)

22. Major Harris (Pittsburgh), standout option quarterback

21. Willie Thrower (New Kensington)—the man with a perfect name for a quarterback—was the first African American to appear in an NFL contest during the modern era, coming off the bench for the Chicago Bears in 1953 to relieve starter (and onetime roommate) George Blanda.

20. Bob Naponic (Greensburg)
19. John Hufnagel (McKees Rocks)
18. Ron Lancaster (Clarion)
17. Tom Clements (McKees Rocks), who led Notre Dame to a national championship
16. Terry Hanratty (Butler), who also excelled at Notre Dame
15. Chuck Fusina (McKees Rocks), the third quarterback on this list from the small borough of McKees Rocks
14. Babe Parilli (Rochester), a two-time consensus All-American out of the University of Kentucky
13. Charlie Batch (Homestead)
12. Richie Lucas (Glassport)
11. Bruce Gradkowski (Pittsburgh)—yet another signal caller from the Steel City

The list is not all inclusive or totally up to date, as the state has produced other stars such as Jeannette's Terrelle Pryor, a National Player of the Year and the first Pennsylvania high school player to produce both run *and* pass yardage totals of 4,000+ yards.

One source itemizes a glut of quarterbacks from their list of the nine most prolific Pittsburgh-area high schools (through May 2011). These boys were, at the least, good enough to have become starters at major colleges for at least the bulk of one season. (See appendix 1 for the entire list of players and their high schools.)

The MaxPreps website came up with its selection of the top 10 quarterbacks from all over the state of Pennsylvania. They wound up with a "Behold this!" moment when they revealed that a stunning 8 of the 10 greatest on their list hailed from the Pittsburgh part of the state, based on players who spent their high school days living within a radius of about 50 miles around the city. Only Ron Powlus (No. 10) and Rich Gannon (No. 8) were from outside that area—meaning that each player in the top 7 came from either Pittsburgh or one of the nearby neighboring towns.

An article by Kevin Askeland on MaxPreps concluded that the best state in America for producing running backs is California, citing men from O. J. Simpson to Marcus Allen and Terrell Davis. Askeland proposed Florida as the best state for cultivating great receivers. At the time of the article, 13 of the top 100 receivers hailed from Florida. Five of them could boast of 10,000+ career yards in receptions, including Isaac Bruce, Michael Irvin, and Anquan Boldin. However, in selecting the premier origination point for elite quarterbacks, Askeland went with Pennsylvania. He listed several men who are not from Western Pennsylvania, including Matt Schaub from (West Chester); Matt Ryan (Exton), who played for William Penn Charter School in Philadelphia; and Kerry Collins (Lebanon) and Chad Henne (Wyomissing), who both played for Wilson High School in West Lawn. However, the majority of the talent was once more packed around Pittsburgh.

Through the end of 2012, a dozen of the top 100 quarterbacks, based on total passing yards, were from Pennsylvania, and five of them have 35,000+ yards. Of that group, only Collins did not hail from around Pittsburgh. The others were Marino, Montana, Unitas, and Kelly.

One ESPN report in 2012 listed the top five states for producing splendid quarterbacks as being Texas, California, Alabama, Ohio, and Pennsylvania. At the time the list was compiled, those five states had produced 15 Heisman Trophy winners, 18 Hall of Famers, and "more than half of the top 100 quarterback prospects in the ESPNU Class of 2012 rankings." In addition, "the talent spans generations, from quarterbacks who are still 17 and 18 years old to veterans whose glory days were 20 or more years ago."

While all five of those states possess impressive QB credentials, none of the other four states can boast the same concentration of quarterback excellence within such a limited geographic area as Western Pennsylvania. Incredibly, by 2005 when Dan Marino entered the Pro Football Hall of Fame, 6 of 22 quarterbacks in the Hall were from the Pittsburgh vicinity (27 percent), the most of any state. Through 2016, the number of modern-era quarterbacks honored in Canton, Ohio, swelled a bit to 26, but that still means the vicinity around the Steel City had produced nearly a whopping one-fourth of all QB Hall of Famers. The illustrious roll call features The Six—Blanda, Unitas, Namath, Montana, Marino, and Kelly—who have each earned a chapter in this book.

In every professional season from 1949 through the turn of the century, at least one of those six men was active, except for the 1978 season. And, boy, were they winners. Combined, their teams took part in 13 of the first 48 NFL Super Bowls, and they even accounted for AFL and NFL titles earlier in the 1950s and into the 1960s.

The Six represents a wildly disproportionate amount of superstar quarterbacks for one state to own, especially considering that the population of Pennsylvania has, of course, never been large enough statistically to account for such domination. For example, at one point not long ago, the population of the state represented only about 4 percent of the nation's total population.

By all logical accounting, absolutely *no* state, let alone a mere slice of a state, should be able to produce one-fourth of all Hall of Fame quarterbacks from the modern era. Furthermore, The Six represented 33 percent of all quarterbacks from the five most productive states identified in the ESPNU report. It was no wonder that the report summarized (and understated) that Western Pennsylvania "has been a breeding ground for some of the nation's best passers."

As writer Carlton Stowers noted, when commentators mull over their picks for the greatest quarterbacks ever, even today they "talk about Montana, [John] Elway, Unitas, [Terry] Bradshaw, [Brett] Favre, and Marino." Half of those men were Pittsburgh products.

Call it a cradle, a factory—or any other metaphor you choose—Western Pennsylvania is the ultimate source for quarterbacks.

2 GEORGE BLANDA
The NFL's Methuselah

SELECT LIFETIME FACTS, statistics, and records of note: Blanda threw for 236 lifetime touchdowns, which remains high on the all-time list at No. 28. In fact, 5.9 percent of his lifetime throws went for scores, representing the 14th best percentage to this day. Blanda is one of just two men to have played in the NFL in four different decades; his 26 seasons represent the longest tenure ever in professional football. Thanks to his passing and kicking abilities, Blanda held the record for scoring in the most consecutive contests and for leading his league in points after touchdowns the most times. Upon his retirement, he had scored more points than any football player ever; until recent years, he remained first on the all-time scoring list. Through 2016, he was still standing at No. 1 for most extra points made.

• • •

Start the discussion of The Six with George Blanda—it only makes sense to do so, not only chronologically, but also because it almost seems as if Blanda himself goes back to the very start of pro football. Sure, that's a stretch, but the ageless Blanda is clearly the logical person to begin the string of Hall of Fame quarterbacks from Western Pennsylvania.

Blanda was the son of a Czech immigrant who found work—dangerous, dirty work at that—as a coal miner. Blanda never forgot his family or his hometown. When he gave his induction speech in 1981, as he entered the Pro Football Hall of Fame, he stated that he was "proud of the fact that I grew up in a very, very small town with a great mom and dad who raised eleven kids in that tradition of playing football in Western Pennsylvania. Proud I grew up in a little town called Youngwood, which was in the heart of football in Western Pennsylvania. I was very proud of my heritage, and I developed a lot of character in the early days and learned that, with hard work, dedication, discipline, tenacity, and never giving up, you can succeed in improving your life."

Incidentally, when Blanda was inducted into the Hall at age 54, author Allan Maki quipped that he "probably had another season or two left in him."

At any rate, coming from a family that gave him six brothers, four sisters, and a competitive spirit nearly unmatched in sports, Blanda readily admitted his background fostered his intensity. "We competed for everything. Even the food on our table."

Mike Ditka felt that "the thing that made George good—now, not that he didn't have talent, he did have talent—he was the greatest competitor. He didn't like to lose in anything. I put him with Jim Harbaugh—he does not like to lose at anything, and that's the way George was. If they played cards or he played golf or he played marbles, he wanted to win. And when you get people who have that initiative and drive, they find a way to make themselves better and to win."

Decades after Blanda's battles for table scraps, Oakland Raiders owner Al Davis described Blanda as a man who "inspired a whole nation" and possessed fires within. According to Davis, the one trait that burned the brightest in Blanda "was the will to win." Davis noted that Blanda "had a God-given killer instinct to make it happen when everything was on the line. He knew how to lead. He knew how to win. I really believe that George was the greatest clutch player that I have ever seen in the history of professional football."

When Coach Bear Bryant came to the University of Kentucky in 1946, Blanda was a sophomore with experience as a blocking back and punter. The Wildcats were coming off a dismal 1–9 season, but the team lost just nine more games over the following three seasons. For two of those years (1947 and 1948), as an upperclassman, Blanda was the quarterback, beginning when Bryant installed what was considered to be the revolutionary T formation offense. The young Blanda hit on almost exactly 50 percent of his throws, while compiling a relatively modest 1,451 yards, with 12 touchdown strikes.

More often than not, Blanda grasped the football in his large hands and, as a "control" passer, threw short passes, "low, flat, fast" ones. His skill and leadership took the Wildcats to two bowl games, including the school's first-ever bowl appearance, a win over Villanova in Blanda's junior season.

From 1949 until the start of the next century, at least one of The Six was active in the NFL with the exception of 1978 (between Joe Namath's retirement and the rookie season of the next baton carrier, Joe Montana). That's a period of 50 out of 51 years with a star Western Pennsylvania quarterback as an NFL fixture, and it all began with George Blanda. In fact, this Methuselah of a quarterback/kicker was responsible for 26 of those seasons (overlapping with Unitas and Namath).

Think about it: Blanda first threw a football as a professional way back in 1949 when Harry Truman was our nation's president and when the flag that fluttered over his White House featured just 48 states. Blanda was still flinging the ball (albeit only three times) in 1975 when Gerald Ford led our country. Of course, Blanda's career ran from the time when all placekickers approached the ball in the traditional way, straight on, to the advent of the European-/soccer-style approach.

Blanda goes back so far, that on the day he was born, September 17, 1927, Babe Ruth was temporarily detoured on his march to a record-setting 60 home runs in a season when he was walked three times. In addition to that, the NFL was in just its sixth season and featured a mere dozen teams, with names such as the Providence Steam Roller, the Duluth Eskimos, the Frankford Yellow Jackets, and the Pottsville Maroons.

Raymond Berry once joked of Blanda, "You need to ask him about the durability pills he took."

Bimbo Cecconi, who starred as a quarterback at Pitt, said that of all the great football stars to come out of Western Pennsylvania, Blanda deserves the title as most versatile. "It's because of his ability to play offense, defense, kick, and for all the points he scored [in many ways]."

Start in Chicago, where Blanda spent the first 10 seasons of his career with the Bears (with the exception of one game with the Colts). Even in 1949, when initially signing with the Bears, Blanda had a deep mistrust and dislike of Coach George Halas, who—as told by Arnold Hano—"instead of a bonus, paid him $600 advance on his salary. Which is the same as saying he lent him $600. That's how you owe your soul to the company store."

In turn, Halas never had full faith in Blanda as his quarterback; one year he actually had Blanda mired fourth on the quarterback depth chart, behind men such as Ed Brown and Zeke Bratkowski, names now familiar only to the best-informed football cognoscenti. In 1949 Blanda began his NFL days as a third-string quarterback, behind legends Johnny Lujack and Sid Luckman—nothing to be ashamed of.

In 1951, after throwing the football only 22 times in his first two seasons, the rugged Blanda also suited up as a starting linebacker and handled placekicking duties as well. The Bears didn't give him the starting quarterback job until 1953, when he led the league in completions and attempts.

However, by 1955, Blanda's quarterbacking skills were again languishing on the bench, where they would remain for the rest of his days in Chicago. Halas was, for the most part, employing him only as his placekicker. From 1956 through 1958, Blanda threw just 95 times. The proud but thwarted Blanda announced his retirement after the 1958 season; in 1959 he became a salesperson for a trucking company. Never afraid of toil, he continued to work for that company in 22 of his record-setting 26 seasons in pro football.

Blanda didn't stay retired for long. The new, upstart American Football League (AFL), which began play in 1960, wanted him and envisioned him under center once more. So, after being idle for just one season, he accepted an offer from the Houston Oilers, giving them, as writer Bob Carroll put it, "in one swoop, . . . a crafty veteran passer and the best placekicker in the league."

Over a 14-game schedule, Blanda won 8 of his 11 starts at quarterback in 1960; his Oilers went 10–4 and then won the first-ever AFL championship. On a balmy New Year's Day in 1961, Houston hosted the Los Angeles Chargers (so named before the team moved for a long stretch to San Diego) in Jeppesen Stadium and upended them, 24–16.

The contest marked Blanda's first postseason win. With the help of three of his receivers, Blanda accounted for every one of his team's 24 points: throwing TD passes to Dave Smith (17 yards), Bill Groman (7 yards), and Billy Cannon (an 88-yard bomb in the fourth quarter); kicking the extra point after each of those scores; and launching a short field goal in the first half. He finished with 16 competitions good for 301 yards.

The Oilers of 1961 couldn't get things going at first, beginning the season 1–3–1. Predictably, Coach Lou Rymkus, somewhat of a martinet, was fired. His replacement, Wally Lemm, was more tolerant and, when it came to his personnel, savvier. Instead of playing two quarterbacks (the other one being the now-forgotten Jacky Lee), he made Blanda his exclusive quarterback and, figuratively, eased into a hammock to watch as his guy guided Houston to a 9–0 record down the stretch, throwing for a league-high 3,330 yards and firing 36 touchdowns for a new professional season record. On one particularly torrid day, Blanda even amassed a stupendous 464 yards through the air. Also, his 9.2 yards per pass attempt in 1961 now places him in a tie for the No. 16 slot for a single season; his 17.8 yards per completion remains No. 12 all-time through the 2016 season. Not only that, 9.9 percent of all Blanda's passes went for touchdowns, which is still the sixth best percentage ever.

In each of his seven seasons in Houston, Blanda led his team in passing and scoring, and he later became the first man to score 500+ points for three teams. Passes from his lethal arm and kicks off his booming leg riddled the air like bullets from a machine gun—or, better yet, given Blanda's age, like spray from a Gatling gun. Not bad for a man who had "retired" several years earlier. For his achievements, Blanda was named the Player of the Year both by the Associated Press and by the United Press International.

The 513 points the Oilers put on the scoreboard also established a professional record. In the process, two of Blanda's receivers also set or tied records: Charley Hennigan set a new standard with 1,746 yards in receptions, and Bill Groman tied Don Hutson's NFL record of 17 touchdowns. Furthermore, Blanda helped Houston accumulate 6,288 yards, when no other team had even sniffed the 6,000-yard plateau. For quite some time, Blanda's December 3, 1961, field goal, which sailed 55 yards, ranked as the second longest three-point kick of all-time (a year later, he came close again with a 54-yarder).

The 1961 AFL title game, held at Balboa Stadium on Christmas Eve, resulted in a 10–3 Houston victory over the Chargers (who had by then settled down in San Diego). Blanda once again accounted, via his right arm and right leg, for all of the Oilers' points, kicking a 46-yard field goal, connecting with Billy Cannon for a 35-yard touchdown strike, and booting the extra point. On the debit side, he threw five interceptions that day. Nevertheless, winning two championships over the AFL's first two seasons was a crowning achievement for the 34-year-old Blanda.

In 1962 Blanda's record was 11–3, and he took Houston to their third successive title game. (He never again won more games than he lost as the *starting* quarterback with the exception of a 1–0 year in 1968.) Unfortunately, in a title game featuring two Texas-based teams, he had 5 of his 46 passes picked off in a 20–17 double-overtime loss to the Dallas Texans.

It was that kind of year as he led the league with 42 interceptions, a new pro record, marking the first of four consecutive years in which he would top the AFL in passes picked off. One out of every 10 passes he threw in the 1962 regular season went to a man wearing the wrong jersey—remember, this occurred just one year after he had led the AFL with 36 TDs. At times in 1962, Blanda was about as effective as a placebo. In fairness, though, he did fire 27 touchdown passes and compiled 2,810 yards.

Reviews on Blanda as a quarterback have been somewhat mixed at times. Fred Cox said: "Blanda was probably the most average [of The Six], even though he was really good. I don't think he was in the same league with Joe Montana and the others. I'm not taking anything away from him; it's just a fact. Blanda's greatest thing that he had going for him was longevity. He played forever and ever, and he was a decent kicker."

The 1963 season ended with his third straight selection as an All-Pro. He accounted for 3,003 yards through the air to once more lead the AFL; this was the first of three years in a row in which he was No. 1 for the most completed passes in the league. However, he lost 7 of the 13 games he started.

The next two seasons he got 13 and 12 starts at the quarterback spot, respectively, before plummeting to just 8 starts the next year, his final one as an Oiler. It was then that Houston placed him on waivers, and the Oakland Raiders obtained him for practically nothing.

In 1967, with Daryle "The Mad Bomber" Lamonica firmly entrenched as the Raiders quarterback, Blanda became his backup. Experts recognized him as the game's best understudy. As such, Blanda did not get his next start, his last one ever, until November 10, 1968. That day he went ballistic. He tossed four touchdown passes, including a 94-yard bomb to Warren Wells, kicked two field goals, and launched five extra points—good enough for the 41-year-old to win the league's Player of the Week award.

For the record, in 1967 and 1968 he didn't throw many passes, but 9 of his 45 completions (20 percent) went for scores. Not only that, in one 1968 game against the Kansas City Chiefs, Blanda established a new Raiders record for accuracy by hitting his target on 11 of his 14 passes. Plus, in 1967 he led the league for the highest success rate on field goal attempts, doing so for the third and final time in his career.

Despite all of his accomplishments, most football fans remember him for one thing: his incredible 1970 season when, as writer Arnold Hano put it, "43-year-old George, a grumpy saint, kept coming off the bench to slay his weekly dragon."

However, there almost wasn't a 1970 season for Blanda. Before the season was to open, and just a few days before his 43rd birthday, he was put on waivers. His pride bashed with the impact of a Larry Wilson full-out safety blitz, Blanda insisted, "I can still throw the ball, and I think I can still call some signals." Finally, Oakland's general manager Al Davis became convinced that young Kenny Stabler could not give the Raiders as much insurance as Blanda, marking the start of Blanda's Lazarus-like revival act. Here was a man who was on a mission to prove something— not to himself, but to Davis and to the world.

On October 25, he replaced an injured Lamonica and fired three TD passes, good for a 31–14 win over the Pittsburgh Steelers. That was merely the beginning of a five-week run that left the football world reeling.

The following Sunday featured a Blanda 48-yard field goal with eight ticks left on the scoreboard, salvaging a tie against Kansas City.

When his Oakland Raiders defeated the Cleveland Browns, 23–20, on November 8, 1970, Blanda didn't enter the game until the final quarter— with just 4:10 left to play and his team trailing, 20–13. He then turned in a memorable performance, not only slinging a pass for a touchdown (with time dwindling down to 1:34), but—once Oakland got the ball back, with the clock down to three seconds—by booting a game-winning field goal from a distance of 52 yards. It was the longest kick he had attempted in his four years with Oakland.

Undeterred by age, he was now well on his way to saving five contests in a row "with his last-minute heroics." The final two victories came in the waning moments of games versus the Denver Broncos (a scoring pass) and the San Diego Chargers (another game-winning kick).

Of the five histrionics-packed games that season, Blanda enjoyed the one against the Browns the most. "I never had so much fun in my life," he grinned. His glee stemmed largely from the fact that the victory allowed him to exact revenge against Cleveland, a team he had never before defeated and one that he despised dating back to the time one of the Browns separated his shoulder, the only major injury of his 26-season career.

A Blanda teammate, George Atkinson, said, "Can you imagine even playing at 43, never mind doing what he did in the 1970 season?" At season's end, Kansas City Chiefs owner Lamar Hunt joked, "Why, this George Blanda is as good as his father, who used to play for Houston."

Over this memorable stretch of dramatics, fans displayed signs and sent correspondence to Blanda with messages such as: "On behalf of all the other senile old wrecks, we salute you!" and, from a banner in the Raiders' home venue, "WELCOME TO THE OLD FOLKS HOME." One writer called his showing the "Blanda Revival Tour."

Blanda himself addressed the age issue: "I don't think age makes any difference when you're a quarterback. . . . Heck, if a quarterback is with the right team, he could play at sixty. The secret to quarterbacking is not throwing passes but play selection, reading defenses, and motivating the team. There are plenty of guys around who can really throw the ball but don't make it because they don't have those other qualities."

While the "revenge-is-mine" win over Cleveland and the entire five-game winning streak were certainly satisfying—as was being named the Player of the Year—those accomplishments were neither the apex nor the end of Blanda's career. He had already finished the 1970 season as the oldest quarterback ever to have played in an NFL title game, when he accounted for all of his team's 17 points in the 1970 AFC championship game loss against the Colts, but there was more. Remarkably, Blanda would continue to toil, mainly as a kicker, until after he had turned 48.

By the end of the 1970 season, Blanda had managed to own or share 37 professional football records, including the most passes thrown and the most passes completed in a single game, most touchdowns in a single season (36, tied then with Y. A. Tittle), and the most touchdowns fired in a game (7, tied then with six other players).

How the chain-smoking, bourbon-sipping old-timer could endure so long can be attributed, wrote Hank Hersch, to, "his upbringing in Youngwood, Pa., where Blanda was toughened up by six brothers and taught the value of hard work by his father, a coal miner."

Tough? No question about it. Blanda once observed of the grueling nature of football: "Sure, pro football is violent. That's one of the nicest things about it." He relished the game's excitement, challenges, and even its contact. "I love the thrill of getting off a pass before getting smashed down," he once stated.

Oakland linebacker Phil Villapiano once observed: "George was never gentle. There were three people on the Raiders whom you were scared of because you knew if you made a mistake they were really going to get on you—[head coach John] Madden, [center] Jim Otto and George Blanda."

Proud and self-confident? Assuredly so. Before the start of his 1970 season of glory, Oakland's managing general partner Al Davis informed Blanda that he had been put on waivers. Davis really had no plans of losing his backup quarterback and was merely making a common strategic front-office move, but Blanda exploded, "This is the worst thing that's ever happened to me!" His anger, it turns out, was not aimed solely at

Davis; he was also furious to learn that every other team had passed on the opportunity to claim him off waivers. He bellowed at Davis, "You've made it very clear to me that you see me as an ancient quarterback on his last legs, and *I'm not*." He wasn't.

On December 21, 1975, Blanda threw three passes, including his final completion in a 28–20 victory over the Chiefs. The following week he accounted for seven points in a playoff win over Cincinnati. Then, on January 4, 1976, in a loss to Pittsburgh, Blanda put four points on the scoreboard, with an extra point and a fourth-quarter field goal, to close out the scoring both in the game and for his career.

Blanda did not manage to play when he was 60, but he came pretty close to remaining active in the league into his 50s—his official retirement came one week before his 49th birthday, in 1976. Incredibly, his career had spanned four decades. Thirty-four years after retiring, time finally caught up with him; he passed away at the age of 83.

If he played today, his stats would even be better than what they were, says Mike Lucci:

> [Blanda] didn't look like he played pretty. I think there was a different generation if you go back to the Blandas—it was more of an instinctive kind of thing. It was more of a street football, and they excelled because they had that inner toughness or that ability to adapt.
>
> The game has evolved. I mean, it's like now you watch Peyton Manning and some [others], and they have made it so that it's not quite as instinctive. It's like, "I'm going to read this, and if this happens, I'm going to do that." He may be the greatest quarterback, he may not be, but I think that back with Blanda, the game was a little different.
>
> Today you can't touch a receiver after he goes five yards. In the old days you could knock the shit out of him all over the field. So if you really thought about it, routes weren't as precise. They had to throw to an open space, but they had to read to see, "Well, is the linebacker going to clothesline this guy and knock him off or grab him and impede his route?" It was more instinctive rather than—I don't know if you want to say reactive—but the game is different.

As great and gritty as Blanda was, it was his perseverance perhaps that most contributed to his entry into the Hall of Fame. Yes, Blanda is a legend—but be aware of one fact (a bit of knowledge that could win a lot of bar bets): His win–loss record for games in which he started at quarterback is not much more than break-even. He won 53, tied 1, and lost 50 of the games in which he started under center.

Nevertheless, tribute must be paid to a man who, like Willie Loman in *Death of a Salesman,* plugged away year after year. Tribute is definitely owed to a man who, upon his retirement, had scored more points (2,002) and played in more professional football games (340) than anyone else. Not only was he ageless—he was also peerless.

JOHNNY UNITAS

The Man with the Golden Arm and a Heart to Match

SELECT LIFETIME STATISTICS, and records of note: Enshrined in the Pro Football Hall of Fame in 1979, Unitas led the NFL in practically every offensive category, including passing yards and touchdown passes (four times in a row, 1957–60), most completions (three times), and passer rating (three times). Bold print, denoting league leadership, adorns his entry in football's all-time registry.

On 17 different occasions, Unitas threw four touchdowns in a game. He fired the football for 290 lifetime touchdowns (still No. 13 all-time) and for a total of 40,239 yards (No. 18). He is still the 11th best quarterback ever, based on lifetime yards gained per pass attempt (7.8); he accounted for 41,426 yards of total offense (No. 15 all-time).

Unitas was the epitome of consistency. From 1956 to 1960, he established a record when he threw for at least one touchdown in 47 straight contests, while averaging just 14.8 completions per game. That set an amazingly durable record that stood until the 2012 season. Over that 47-game span, he threw 102 touchdowns.

In a 1969 poll conducted by the NFL, Unitas was selected as the greatest player of the league's first 50 years. He was also the Player of the Decade for the 1960s. Little wonder: he was a ten-time Pro Bowler, a first-team All-Pro five times, and the league MVP in 1959, 1964, and 1967.

In 1994, a committee of media and NFL personnel selected Unitas and Montana (along with Sammy Baugh and Otto Graham) as their quarterbacks when they came up with their all-time 75th anniversary team. Five years later, *Sports Illustrated* voted Unitas the second best quarterback ever (behind Montana) and the fifth best player in NFL annals.

Upon the completion of his career, he held 22 records and did so while playing in only 211 regular season games.

• • •

Start with his toughness, then trace it back to his youth, and a picture of Johnny Unitas begins to emerge quite clearly. Perhaps the one story that portrays his stoutheartedness is the one his teammate, All-Pro Andy Nelson, relates so well: "Once Unitas got a broken nose, and I remember him stuffing some mud up his nose to keep it from bleeding. Then he threw a touchdown pass to Lenny Moore. He was a tough character. That's how he earned our respect—he played with injuries."

Hall of Famer Gino Marchetti recalled an incident from a 1960 game when the Baltimore Colts traveled to Chicago: "It was probably the roughest game that I ever played in, and probably for John, too. He really took a beating, and Jim Parker felt bad because Doug Atkins was giving Parker fits, and I can remember coming off the sideline and sitting next to John. God, he was bleeding, his nose, he looked terrible."

That is when Colts coach Weeb Ewbank told Unitas he was going to pull him from the game. Marchetti continued: "John looked at him straight in the eye and said, 'Listen, you are not taking me out. If you take me out, I'll kill you.' John could have easily taken a couple of plays off and nobody would have said anything, but he didn't want to do that. He said a quarterback is the leader of the offense and he wanted to lead, and that's exactly what he did." He not only stayed in the Bears game, he won it on a late touchdown pass to Moore.

Nelson added, "Back in those days, players would get a concussion and they'd put smelling salts under your nose and hold up fingers and send you back in. The thing was to play through it. At the end of his career, he was in pretty much pain. His fingers had been broken and they were going every which way."

Paige Unitas called her father "crazy tough." She said: "He never complained, ever. When he started losing the feeling in his right arm, couldn't pick things up, or button his shirt or cut his steak, he never let it frustrate him." Instead of, say, throwing down his utensils in frustration, he would simply say, "I have a left hand," or, "That's why God gave me two hands." According to Paige, "he would make do with what he had, and he still signed autographs for hours and never complained; and it couldn't have been comfortable. I think his issues with his hand and arm was just another, 'All right, I got to deal with it. No problem.' His hand was almost turned in. It was on an angle, but the signature was still perfect."

Another time, about a year before his death, Unitas was in a hospital; when Paige questioned him about his health, he complained a bit, but mainly downplayed it. "It was almost crazy," she commented of his stoicism, but added: "When he's saying something is a *little* off, [it's bad]. And it got worse until he said, 'Jesus, Mary, and Joseph, this thing is killing me. Can you get the nurse?' If *you're* telling me to get the nurse, this has gone 10 times crazier than [what most people could endure]." It turned out he had a blood clot moving up his leg, yet he had somehow remained relatively calm.

Paige related a similar story about her father when he was young. "He shot right through his finger with, I think, a BB gun. My Aunt Shirley took him to the trolley and took him to . . . a doctor. She said he never said a word the whole time. Later he said, 'It wasn't real uncomfortable.' Really? You almost shot your finger off! He had a crazy amount of pain tolerance."

Sandy Unitas recalled a time she and her husband lived on a farm: "There was many a time when there was ice and snow and he would need something from the barn. He would put his clothes on and walk all the way out there. I'd say, 'Why didn't you get one of the kids to do it?' He was concerned about his leg, and he'd say, 'If you don't use it, you'll lose it,' and he just kept pushing and pushing and pushing himself. He had very high pain tolerance."

On one occasion, he hid his agony from his wife overnight, and the following day, while driving, he suddenly pulled over and asked her to drive. Subsequently, after initially balking at her pleas to see a doctor, he gave in, and she rushed him to the hospital. "If he asked me to drive him, I *knew* something was wrong. Having such a high pain tolerance was not necessarily beneficial to him late in life—maybe it was when he was playing. He was not a complainer."

Paige's brother Joe said Unitas got his toughness from his mother, "and from the times that he grew up in. Once he had had a good game in high school. It was a cold, rainy, Pittsburgh fall day and he came home feeling pretty good about himself, and his mother told him that one of the ladies up the street had a bunch of coal in the front of her house and he needed to make sure it got shoveled down the coal chute into her basement. His response was, 'I just got home and it's raining outside.' She didn't care. She said, 'I know that it's raining. See that it gets done.'"

Paige recalls the family tale a bit differently, but the bottom line was the same: When Johnny displayed his reluctance to do his job, saying he was exhausted, his mother shot back, "I didn't ask if you were tired or not. What I said was, 'You need to go down the hill and put coal in her [bin].' When you come home, you do what you need to do—get it done." Lesson taught.

No question, his family influenced him greatly. Unitas's father Francis, a hard-working man, was just 37 years old when he passed away of kidney failure, leaving behind a coal-delivery business; his wife, Helen (née Superfisky); and children, including a sad five-year-old Johnny. Following Francis's death, during the Great Depression, Helen had to work as many as three jobs to provide for her children.

John Ziemann, deputy director of the Sports Legends and Babe Ruth Birthplace Museum, said, "His parents were Lithuanian, and they came from an environment of hard workers. I think that's what made John survive—it was a tough life, and a life that taught him that you have to get out and work for what you want."

Leonard Unitas, the oldest child, six years older than John, said, "I was more of his Pap than his brother. My father died and there was four of us—I was the oldest, I was 11. Somebody had to take care of them. There wasn't too much money around and because I was the oldest one, I was the one that got him his shoes and whatever else he needed."

Unitas's wife, Sandy, said: "There were several family members who offered to take one of the children, but [Unitas's mother] said that she would not let that happen. She would work to keep them together. They had a nice home which she had to sell and move to another neighborhood. John really admired her for that."

Shirley Green, 16 months younger than her brother John, said: "He was very quiet. He didn't have a temper." Later the two never spoke of his football playing. "That was a different part of his life." Football took a backseat to family and religion. "With him, what you saw is what you got—he had nothing grand about him. He was as down to earth as could be."

When her father was recruited by the University of Louisville, Paige Unitas recounted, "My grandmother listened [to the recruiters], then interrupted, 'I don't really care about all this stuff that you're saying. You have to answer two [conditions] for me then you can have him—that he's going to graduate and that he goes to church every Sunday.' They said, 'Yes, ma'am,' and that's all she needed to know. She said, 'He's all yours.'"

Unitas carried his mother's views and values into his role as a father. Paige noted:

> She was wonderful and loving but tough. She had to be; and my parents were very open and honest. "Tell us what you're doing, but if you lie, you know your ass is in trouble."

He was very to the point. He got mad at me, he grounded me, he didn't let me do things I wanted to do, just like any dad, but he was just known and loved by the whole world.

He was very generous and very kind and very straightforward. If you messed up, you knew, and there really was no getting out of it. He wasn't going to yell at you, he never yelled—there was never any yelling or screaming. It was very much like, "You messed up, you know you did it, you know what's going to happen." And that's the end of the discussion. We didn't have discussions. His mother was very much like that—they were all kinda cut from the same mold.

Paige remembered other lessons passed down from her grandmother to her father and then to her:

He would tell us, because we were all very athletic and played every-thing, "There's no complaining. Don't come off the field and sit there and say another teammate didn't execute. No, you messed up. You're the one who messed us up, what are you trying to blame another person for?"

The people would expect him to be this hard-nosed, "you-gotta-be-number-one" person, but, no. He always said do the best that you can do and have fun.

Chad saw his father as a no-frills, get-the-job-done kind of man. "That was him," he laughed. "He didn't want to hear any 'what-ifs' or 'I can't do this' or 'I can't do that.' Just get in there and do what you have to do, and get it done. 'I don't want to hear any excuses.'"

Unitas, then, was tough but tender, and that combination made him a great father. Chad Unitas, now an account executive for the Baltimore Ravens, said that his father was his best friend:

You have your father–son relationship, and then you have your best friend relationship, I had both of them combined into one—whether it was playing golf with him all the time or him helping me with dif-ferent sports or life in general. A lot of people call him the greatest quarterback who ever lived, and I always refer to him as the greatest father that ever lived—he was just an unbelievable person.

My older brother Joe and I would always play football in the back-yard, and dad was always the all-time quarterback. He was just my dad is the way I looked at it—he was great at what he did, yeah, but he was the person that I looked up to, idolized, wanted to be like. He was just a wonderful, wonderful father is what it comes down to.

Former teammate Sam Havrilak related a story Unitas had told him about Chad when he was young and not so perceptive: "Chad, who never saw John play, was a quarterback for a local high school here in the Baltimore area. He was having some trouble in practice pitching the ball out. John asked him, 'Well, why don't you come out in the backyard and we'll work on it a little bit.' So Chad showed him how his coach wanted him to pitch the ball out to the running back. John says, 'Why don't you do it this way, it's a little better and a little easier.' Chad said, 'The coach doesn't want me to do it that way.' And John says, 'Yeah, but this is a better way.' And Chad says, 'Well what do you know about it anyway?' John probably kind of just looked at him."

Paige said her father "did so many things for us. Gosh, one time when I was, maybe a sophomore in high school. I needed to go shopping for a new computer and new shoes, and he said, 'I'll take you shopping.' We had a day, just the two of us, but of course the whole time people are coming up to him. He was so gracious always, and I knew it just came with the territory." Meanwhile, he was torn between two things: "He wanted to be with me, but it was funny because everybody was like, 'Do you know who that man is over there?' I said, 'I do. He's really nice. I call him Dad.'"

Later they went out to dinner, and Unitas held open a door for an older gentleman who was using a walker. Paige remembers: "The man stopped and said, 'Young man, I remember watching you, and you brought me a lot of happiness.' My dad said [to me], 'Just go on in and get a table, I'll be right in.' Dad comes back a couple of minutes later, and I said, 'What were you doing?' He said, 'I wanted to help that man to the car. I didn't want him to have a heart attack. I wanted to make sure he got to the car safely.' But the man wouldn't let his hand go when he was shaking it."

For Paige, one story stands out above the rest:

He was doing a signing and this guy came and got [a picture autographed]. He said, "It's actually for my father. He's in a hospice. I wanted to get this for him because he just loves you and, unfortunately, he's really sick. He won't be here too much longer." My dad said, "OK, I hope your father hangs in there," and that's all the guy ever said.

Of course, my dad knew [the dying man's] first name because he had signed the picture. Later that day he went to the hospice and asked where this man was. He sat down with him for two hours and just talked. Now, this man had dementia and Alzheimer's really bad. A couple of hours later, the son shows up with the signed picture. The man was excited and told his son, "I met him today. He came here to see me." And the son is thinking, "Oh, Lord, he's really losing it."

The dying man persisted, "He really came here and talked to me all afternoon," prompting the son to approach a nurse and ask her, "Who came to visit my dad today?" The nurse replied, "Johnny Unitas, and he stayed for two hours." The man passed away that night.

Five days before Unitas died, he was walking with John Ziemann in Baltimore when they spotted a homeless person. Ziemann extended five dollars to him at about the same time the man spied Unitas, "You're John Unitas," he stammered. "Yes, I am, sir," replied Unitas. The homeless man then looked down at his hand, wiped it clean on his shirt, extended it to Unitas and asked if he would shake his hand. Unitas said, "I'd be honored to shake your hand." They engaged in conversation for a good 15 minutes with Ziemann still standing by, five-dollar bill in hand. The homeless person finally broke away, never having taken the money, saying to Unitas, "You take care of yourself, OK?" A moment later Ziemann told Unitas, "You know what? You did a lot for that man. You made him very happy." Unitas reflected, then said, "Maybe they put me on this earth to do that besides play football."

Some of his sterling traits came from his devout Catholic faith background. Andy Nelson said that during training camp Unitas "used to get up every morning, early in the morning, to go to mass. He was proud of the discipline he was brought up with."

Paige said he raised the family to know that going to church each Sunday was a given. "Once the Colts were [on the road], and they had a Saturday night team meeting. They said, 'John, do you have anything to say,' and he said, 'Not really. Mass is at 7:00.' That's all he said, he didn't say you have to come, you need to show up, but the whole team ended up at church at 7:00 on game day. Half of them weren't Catholic, and even a Jewish teammate showed up. When questioned why he was there, he replied, 'I don't know, John said so.'"

Unitas was so loved and looked up to by teammates that even a subtle suggestion became the law. In fact, years later, teammates would relate to Paige that they simply did what he told them to do. She always replied, "*Oh,* I know."

"He was extremely tolerant," continued Paige, "and he never changed. All the [celebrities] nowadays are so different—they get some money and they go nuts, or not even money, just the fame, and they lose their heads. He never, ever, did that."

To many Unitas was a god, but he himself harbored no such delusions. Paige commented: "Dad was humble and he never thought a thing about who he was or what he had done. To him it was his job. That's how he made money. All the stuff that came after that, all the celebrity and all those things, he accepted it because it was part of what he had become, but that wasn't his thing. He didn't need to be out in the public running around shouting who he was. He would rather be sitting at home, having a beer, watching football in his chair, or mowing the lawn."

John's sister Shirley concurred: "He didn't tell stories about football. That was what he did. That's not who he was. It was a job, but a job that he loved." And Leonard recalled a writer who stated, "One thing about John, no matter how much success he had, he always still wore the same size hat."

Paige said her father put family ahead of personal recognition. Unitas would attend commemorative functions often, feeling that, if someone took the time to honor him, he should go.

So when we'd go to an event, Dad was very much the family man. He wanted everyone to be together. We all knew that you go to these events, don't expect to be hanging with him all night, because it's not going to happen. He's going to be with everybody else in the room, but he handled it so well and was very gracious—tried to talk to everyone and do what he needed to do; then he'd come back and sit with us and we'd have dinner. Even though he knew he'd be bothered every two seconds, he still would sit down and we'd have dinner, we'd be together.

Or when we were with him [around others], he'd say, "This is my daughter Paige. Have you met her," or "This is my son Chad, my wife

Sandy." He'd engage everybody and he wanted people to know this is my family—he's more proud of having his family than what he did. Because, again, to him he didn't really do anything that great—he went to work.

The Unitas family had season tickets to the Baltimore Ravens, watching games from the sidelines. John began to view games as having more sizzle than substance.

He would say, "Do you want to go to that Broadway production on Sunday?" That's kind of what it became—it was a big show, but he enjoyed that we enjoyed it, it got us excited as little kids. He would be happy sitting at home watching on TV.

What was cool was we would be sitting there and the crowd would start chanting, "Unitas." It would get louder and louder and my dad would lean over and say, "You know Paige, you really should greet your fans." So I'd turn around and wave and, of course, nothing. I'd tell him, "I think you should try and see what happens." And he'd turn and as soon as he just put his hand up, cameras are on him, he's on the Jumbotron and 80,000 people are going nuts. He'd smile and wave, then say, "I think you were right."

Sometimes you had to do things to get him excited. Mom had this beautiful trophy room [set up for her husband], and my dad said, "Whatever your mom wants to do is fine." It was done so beautifully with the lighted shelving and all the awards. I'd go in there when he'd call me in to say, "Why'd you spend so much on this credit card?" And I'd explain, then I would say, "Do you ever sit back and look at all this stuff in here? Do you ever for one minute think, 'I'm really cool and this is really cool with all this stuff?'" He was like, "What? What are you talking about?" I said, "Don't you ever look at what you accomplished?" He said, "Paige, I don't need all this stuff. I have the memories."

Paige said that for her father, an ultimate team player, "it was always about the team, it was never about him. He said, 'We wouldn't have this team and be well known if it wasn't for everybody.' It wasn't about him, *ever,* but, of course, everybody else made it about him."

Unitas loved and took care of his fans, signing endless autographs, even when he was eating out. "So many people say to me, 'What was it like with him?' I'm like, 'Probably pretty similar to your father except it took us longer to go to dinner.'"

Unitas even possessed a dry sense of humor as an adult. Once after he had retired, he posed for a picture holding one of his old helmets. He was asked, "What are all these scratches and marks on your helmet?" He quipped, "That's from people not doing their job."

Sandy Unitas told a touching tale that displayed her husband's kindness and thoughtfulness. "I went with John one time to visit a little boy who was dying of cancer. And when I left the room, I said to John, 'There's no way I could ever do this again.' He would do that, but it hurt him so bad, knowing these children were going to die." He continued to make such visits even though each trip tore him up, nearly breaking his heart of gold.

The Johnny Unitas saga is one of dogged determination. He happens to bear the same middle name, Constantine, as the emperor whose victory at the Milvian Bridge was labeled as "among the most decisive moments in world history." Actually, he was given the middle name after his uncle, who was a priest, but in a way it fits: in his own right, Unitas was responsible for what many call the most dramatic victory in NFL history, the Baltimore Colts' 1958 championship win over the New York Giants. Those who remembered him being cut by his first pro team might have considered such a victory to be as impossible as performing an act of alchemy, but Unitas always believed in himself.

His younger cousin Joe Unitas stated, "When he was 12 years old, he knew he wanted to play pro football." Ziemann said, "When he was in school, maybe sixth or seventh grade, he had a strong crush on his teacher. She said to every kid, 'What do you want to be when you grow up?' John said, 'I want to be a quarterback.' So he knew from the beginning what he wanted."

He began his playing days at Catholic (class B) St. Justin's High School. Before Unitas's junior season, says Leonard Unitas, a couple of incompetent coaches had run the team and used John as a receiver; then "Max Carey came in and sort of took John under his wing. He saw the potential in John . . . and had him at first string right off the bat." Unitas was starring by his junior year, often displaying his patented over-the-middle jump pass.

In his biography *Johnny U.,* Tom Callahan wrote that Carey told Unitas, "It's your job to call the plays, but when you come over to me afterward, you damn sure better have a good reason for everything you did."

In his senior year, he repeated as the first-team All-Catholic league quarterback, ahead of Dan Rooney, the son of the Pittsburgh Steelers owner. Joe Unitas said, "St. Justin's was a little, nothing school. Toward the end of his high school career, everybody wanted to go see this kid from St. Justin's who could just throw the heck out of the ball."

Western Pennsylvania is heavily populated by Roman Catholics. As Carlton Stowers wrote in his book *Staubach,* Notre Dame was seen as "the storied university where most young Catholic schoolboys dreamed of one day playing," so the Pittsburgh high schools–to–Notre Dame pipeline of talent was a natural. Unitas also favored the college because he was a fan of Western Pennsylvania's Johnny Lujack, a star for the Irish.

Joe Unitas said, "He didn't have the academics to get to the [schools] that he wanted to go to. Notre Dame was his dream school, and he actually got a tryout there, but they said he was too small." Unitas stood 5'11" and weighed just 137 pounds. Joe said, "He was [fairly] tall, but pretty skinny. He could hide behind a split rail fence pole."

Paige could relate to that description. "I think in high school, as a freshman, he was *so* skinny, really tiny. Everybody thought they were going to kill him." He would eventually fill out and reach 6'1" and around 195 pounds, a weight he pretty much maintained for the rest of his life.

Later in life, Unitas owned a farm, and the image of Unitas the farmer was in some ways apt. In 1959, when Colts teammate Alex Hawkins first spotted Unitas in the locker room, he observed, "Here was a total mystery. [Unitas] was from Pennsylvania, but he looked so much like a Mississippi farmhand that I looked around for a mule. He had stooped shoulders, a chicken breast, thin bowed legs and long, dangling arms with crooked, mangled fingers."

Former Colt Tom Matte saw beyond that and said Unitas had very big hands, an asset for a quarterback. "Unitas's fingers were like an inch-and-a-half longer than mine. He could wrap his hands almost all around the football." Likewise, Colts teammate Havrilak was cognizant that looks aren't everything, saying, "If you look at today's players, obviously they work out, they take supplements, none of that was available back when he started. So he really didn't look like a football player, but he had great football skills, obviously, and he had a great football mind."

However, some college coaches could not get beyond his appearance. The University of Pittsburgh, which was on the receiving part of an endless torrent of athletic talent from the Steel City's vicinity; Notre Dame, which also plucked many a Western Pennsylvania star; and Indiana University all passed on Unitas, who then went to Louisville. Ziemann said, "Great arm, but none of the colleges wanted him."

Diminutive size and rural appearance notwithstanding, Unitas played both ways at Louisville, wearing No. 16. Some early Louisville highlights included his showing in his first start, which took place in the Cardinals' fifth game of the 1951 season versus St. Bonaventure. Unitas hit on 11 consecutive passes, 3 for touchdowns. The Louisville squad sported a 5–4 record in his freshman year, with four straight wins concluding the season. Unitas even helped engineer an improbable win as Louisville topped Houston, favored by 19 points coming into the game, 35–28. He fired four touchdowns, with one TD pass going for 93 yards, still good for a Louisville record. However, that season was his only winning one at the school.

"After his freshman year," said Joe Unitas, "the school kind of deemphasized football [stressing academics instead] so a lot of the guys on the team didn't have the grades to stay on the team. So the coach told them that they were going back to two-way football. So he played safety. Because they were so bad, he ended up making most of the tackles." At times he even returned kickoffs.

In his sophomore season, 1952, the squad was down to 19 players, so they brought in some walk-on freshmen to fill out the roster. Now recognizing his talent, Indiana tried to lure Unitas away, but he stayed loyal to the only team that had wanted him.

Overmatched by a score of 59–6 in one game versus Tennessee, Unitas ran for 52 yards, returned six kickoffs for 85 yards, and ran back a punt as well. In that game he was said to have made 86 percent of his team's tackles. For all of his accomplishments, he became the first—and so far the *only*—Louisville football player to have his jersey number retired.

Still, some of his *collegiate* numbers, while certainly good, were not quite jaw dropping. As a senior, Unitas put the ball up just 110 times and completed only 44 passes for a mere 527 yards and just 3 touchdowns. In his defense, this was during an injury-plagued season, and he was playing in a much different era than today's game. Overall, from 1951 through 1954, he completed 245 passes for 3,139 yards and 27 touchdowns. Looking at it coldly, perhaps it's not exactly shocking that he was still available in the ninth round of the 1955 NFL draft—*still*, 101 players went ahead of him, which in hindsight does seem slightly ludicrous.

Further, it's not like he didn't have talent in college. Andy Nelson, who later became a Colts teammate of Unitas, played against him at Louisville once. "I knew he was good before he came to Baltimore—he completed about 20 passes against us [Memphis State]. A string bean, skinny guy throwing that ball all over the place—I thought, 'Who the hell is that?'"

After leaving the campus of Louisville in 1955, Unitas was drafted by the Pittsburgh Steelers. Some believe the Steelers, who offered him a $5,500 contract for the season, only made their belated ninth-round selection of Unitas because he was a local product. He was also advised not to spend the money right away because his salary was contingent upon his making the team.

Unitas was listed at a lowly fourth slot on the quarterback depth chart, behind Jim Finks, Ted Marchibroda, and Vic Eaton, who was drafted 24 slots behind Unitas. It didn't take long for the Steelers to cut Unitas unceremoniously—he never made it out of training camp. In fact, as hard as it is to believe in retrospect, the coaching staff didn't even take a look at him in any exhibition games: he never took a single snap in any of their contests. When he was cut, he took the last bit of money owed to him and a bus ticket, then cashed in the bus ticket and thumbed his way back to his home.

Much later, someone reminded Marchibroda that Pittsburgh kept him over Unitas. He smiled, "Tell Baltimore they owe me, I did them a favor."

Clearly, the Steelers horribly misjudged Unitas. Kevin Cook wrote that Steelers head coach Walt Kiesling actually believed Unitas "was too dumb to play quarterback in the pros."

Unitas once told Ziemann, "I never minded being cut by the Steelers, but they never gave me a chance."

Vince Dooley said, "I think what's amazing is the number of quarterbacks that most of these professional scouts, with all the knowledge and technology [at their disposal], miss—like Unitas."

Set adrift by Pittsburgh, Unitas was reduced to playing for the Bloomfield Rams, a semipro team, which paid him a measly $6 per game, the minimum salary, until he worked his way up to the maximum of $15 per game. To augment that income and to support himself and his young (first) wife, Dorothy, he also took work in a steel mill running a pile driver. At Bethlehem Steel, he worked alongside men who would later turn out for games to cheer him on.

The Rams played their games each Thursday at the Arsenal Street School in what was called the Greater Pittsburgh League. Their dirt field was shabby; "the players had to get out and sprinkle it with oil before every game to keep the dust down," and the crowds never numbered more than a few hundred fans. Writer Allan Maki stated the field was even "strewn with rocks and shattered glass."

In his book *The Golden Age of Pro Football*, Mickey Herskowitz quoted Unitas as saying, "I was making a hundred twenty-five a week on my job and we were still living with the in-laws, so we weren't starving. But what I needed was the chance to prove that I could play football. The six dollars that I gave to Dorothy every week was important, not because I had earned it but because I had earned it playing *football*."

Wearing No. 45, befitting his defensive back position rather than his role as a quarterback, Unitas was truly earning the meager six dollars by playing both ways for the Rams.

Joe Unitas said things didn't come easy for his father at Bloomfield. "He wasn't really welcomed there by a lot of the guys who were on the team because he had a college education and he had tried to play with Pittsburgh before getting cut. These were some pretty tough and rugged individuals and they beat him up pretty good. The best thing about that was he never said a word; he let his actions prove that he could play rather than trying to go in there and be a loudmouth. He was always telling us if you're good at something, your actions will prove it and people will talk about it; you don't have to tell them about it."

Perhaps Unitas inadvertently alienated some of his Bloomfield teammates when he told them that he would spend the next season in the NFL. "It must have seemed comical," Unitas later reflected, "for a six dollar a game quarterback on the sandlots to be talking about playing with the Steelers or Browns."

Unitas remained unperturbed; he later stated, "I never let stuff bother me. Just growing up the way I did in the street, or working at home. If you had a problem you looked it in the eye and resolved it. We did what we had to do. . . . We didn't panic." His words sounded like lines meant to be delivered by rugged actor John Wayne. Baltimore sportswriter John Steadman succinctly stated that Unitas was "beyond intimidation."

The following season, 1956, the Baltimore Colts did show interest in Unitas after getting an anonymous letter from what was, some people contend, a fan in Pittsburgh (although Baltimore coach Weeb Ewbank often joked he thought Unitas himself had authored the letter), glowing about Unitas's skills. Paige said there was also another man who advised the Colts, "You gotta see this kid in Pittsburgh. He's scrawny, he's lanky, he looks like the water boy, but he can throw." She said they always joked about "how little he was when he first came in," but not for long.

The Colts, in need of a reserve quarterback, gave Unitas a call and an invitation to a tryout camp. They eventually signed the future Hall of Famer for a paltry $7,000. The highest salary the man who would be named the Quarterback of the Century ever pulled down as a Colts player was $125,000.

Writer Robert Smith likened Unitas to a Horatio Alger figure, "who came into professional football, not on the end of a six-figure bonus but of a sixty-cent phone call, asking him if he was still looking for work." More than simply needing work, he craved an opportunity to prove himself.

Carroll Rosenbloom, owner of the Colts, said that not long after the Colts acquired Unitas he received a phone call from Steelers owner Art Rooney. Rosenbloom related, "He said, 'Carroll, you have that boy Uni-TASS. I want to tell you something. My boys tell me that guy was the best looking quarterback we had in camp and my coach never let him *throw* the ball.' After that I watched John throw in practice. He was so relaxed, so loose, and a very likable kid."

Unlike Rooney, Baltimore coach Ewbank defended his Pittsburgh counterpart's ill-fated decision. "A lot of people gave Pittsburgh hell for letting him go, but the fact is they had two good quarterbacks there at the time and, according to [Steelers assistant coach] Herman Bell, the kid hadn't played well."

Ewbank said the first thing he and his staff noticed about Unitas in the spring of 1956 was "the way he followed through, it was exceptional. . . . His arm went through so far that he turned his hand over like a pitcher. I often wondered how he kept from injuring his arm, because it was like throwing a screwball, and all those guys would end up with crooked arms. When he followed through, his fingers turned over and you could see the back of his hand. . . . I worried that he might get what they call a tennis elbow, but, boy, I saw the way he could throw and I never bothered him about it. You knew right away. He was in camp no time at all and we knew that as soon as he learned the offense he would be our quarterback."

In one intrasquad game prior to the exhibition season Unitas hit Raymond Berry for a 51-yard touchdown pass that had a lot of touch on it. Ewbank commented, "A lot of guys can throw deep; Unitas can *pass* deep."

Much later Ewbank would pay an even higher compliment to his star. "I taught John quite a bit the first couple of years. . . . Then he started to teach me."

When starter George Shaw was injured in the second game, against the Chicago Bears, Johnny U. entered the contest with his Colts up, 21–20. The start of his pro career was far from being auspicious. Contrary to a widely believed report, his first NFL pass was not picked off and run back for a score—but that account isn't far from being true. In reality, his first throw was an incompletion, but his second, though not run back for a touchdown, did result in an interception. In the fourth contest of the 1956 season—the first game in which he saw serious action, after throwing just the two passes in the second game—he threw an interception that was returned 59 yards for a score, putting the Bears on top, 27–21, and he fumbled three times, which led to two more scores, in a 58–27 drubbing of Baltimore.

After the fiasco, Rosenbloom made his way down to the locker room, where the stoical Unitas sat, still in uniform, a forlorn figure. Rosenbloom recounted how Unitas "had his head hanging down between his legs so that all you could see was the top of that crew cut. I walked over and got him under the chin and lifted his head up. I said, 'Now, look, John, that was not your fault. You haven't had an opportunity to play and no one is blaming you. You're not only going to be a good one in this league, you're going to be a *great* one." It took some time, though. As a rookie, he threw 9 scores, while 10 of his 198 passes were picked off.

The way Berry saw the emergence of Unitas was insightful, as he observed that Ewbank had been a student of Cleveland coach Paul Brown, who was the brains behind using

[a] simple, sound offense, which Weeb brought to Baltimore. But Brown called the plays for Cleveland [not the quarterback]. Ewbank had been brought up in a system watching the head coach do that. Well, whenever Ewbank saw this free agent Unitas in training camp and saw him throwing the ball and getting the feel for him as a competitor and a football player, [things changed].

Shaw was our starting quarterback and John was just a backup. Well, when George got his terrible knee injury and ended his career with the Colts, Unitas came in to play his first NFL game. Weeb let him call the plays and he instinctively knew that this guy had what it took to do that. That was the key to it—Weeb understanding that Unitas was a natural play caller and a leader. What he delegated to him was a loaded six-shooter with about four bullets in it.

Perhaps the weapon wasn't fully loaded at first, but Unitas had gone from being an NFL reject to being a trusted commodity, one who connected on 55.6 percent of his passes as a rookie, the best percentage by a first-year man in the 37-year history of the NFL. Berry continued, "If it hadn't been for Ewbank, neither one of us would even have had a pro career."

Perseverance and sheer talent prevailed. Unitas rapidly improved, and Shaw—like Wally Pipp, who sustained an injury that took him out of the New York Yankees lineup, to be replaced permanently by baseball immortal Lou Gehrig—soon came to realize he had lost his starting job for good.

Smith wrote that Unitas "listened respectfully to his coach and took charge on the field by his calm, authoritative manner" and that, while on the field, Unitas "was as relaxed as if he were playing touch football in a school playground."

Havrilak stated: "I've always said that there are some quarterbacks who are wired the right way, and they can look at the field and the defense and envision everything going on in their minds while it's going on. There are few people who are able to do that, especially quarterbacks. If you have the ability to do that, and you know where everybody is on the field, it actually makes the game pretty easy, and the game actually slows down quite a bit because the jump from college football to professional football, from a speed level, is just tremendous—only the best play professional football."

Unitas, of course, played pro football like few others ever did. He became a mechanical man, productive and reliable. In his book *When the Grass Was Real,* Bob Carroll wrote, "He was blue-collar all the way. Each year he showed up the first day of camp, did his work every day, and went home after the season. Had there been a time clock at the 50-yard-line, he'd have punched it."

Writer John Patrick pointed out that Unitas didn't take long to become known for his "classic form, instinct and ability to hit both his deep men and short receivers with consistently damaging passes." Patrick also noted that Unitas worked so diligently with receivers such as Raymond

Berry and Jimmy Orr that "he knew where they would be on a pattern without even looking." He concluded his tribute of Unitas by stating how the quarterback's deceptive pump fakes puzzled defenses for years. "John pumps in one direction, looks the other way and then hits the area the defense has just vacated."

Linebacker Mike Lucci agreed, "The first time I was on the field with him I saw Berry, and he would go down 10 yards and break out and the ball would be right there. And they would do it over and over and over again. You always thought, 'He's going to make you pay if you make a mistake.'"

Lucci had great admiration for the precision and timing, despite the fact that Unitas was hampered by the rules of the day, so different than today's. "You could not only grab receivers, you could hit them again at 8 yards or 10 yards as long as the ball wasn't in the air. It was more disruptive."

Two of Unitas's teammates agreed. Raymond Berry said that linemen today hold on so many plays, throwers have much more time than Unitas had. Marchetti said, "First of all, he's the best, and I think if they had the same rules today as they had yesteryear, he would be a much higher rated passer than he is now. Nowadays, a receiver goes down the field and you can't touch him."

Handicaps and hindrances aside, in his first full season as a starter, 1957, Unitas came of age. He reversed the Colts' 5–7 record from the year before and led the NFL in seven categories: pass attempts; touchdowns, averaging two per game; percentage of his passes that resulted in touchdowns (8 percent); quarterback rating (88.0); yards gained per game played (212.5); yards passing (2,550); and yards gained per pass attempt (8.5).

Those are remarkable stats, as are his career numbers, especially considering Unitas played 12- and 14-game regular season schedules, never playing in a season of 16 contests. "So he didn't have the [same] opportunity as today's quarterbacks," said Marchetti.

Asked his opinion about this, Unitas's son Chad chuckled, then commented:

I'm sure there would have been a lot more yards and all that type of stuff. You didn't have as many games as they do now, so, obviously, the records for quarterbacks are going to be a lot more yards now than they were back then.

I mean, that's why it's very hard to compare quarterbacks nowadays with the quarterbacks who were back in the 1950s and 1960s. It's really not comparing apples to apples. One: the rules were different—back then you could do whatever you wanted to the quarterback or the wide receivers, for that matter; nowadays you can't get anywhere near the quarterback and you can't touch the receiver after five yards. Back then, throwing the football 15, 20 times a game was considered a lot. Now they do that in the first half or first quarter.

It's different, but it's the way the league is moving—there's nothing wrong with it, it's just a totally different game than what it was.

To illustrate Chad's point, consider this: Over Tom Brady's last three games leading up to the 2013 AFC championship contest, his 75 passes thrown represented the fewest passes attempted over any three-game span of his entire career. The most passes Unitas ever threw in a year were 436, while Matthew Stafford set a new season record in 2012 when he launched the football 727 times.

The 1958 season for Unitas and his champion Colts was, quite simply, stupendous. After rambling to a 9–3 record and a ticket to the championship, Unitas was named MVP in the title game versus the Giants. Held three days after Christmas, many experts consider that contest to be the greatest NFL game ever played, featuring 15 future Hall of Famers (12 players and 3 coaches). If for no other reason, it was noteworthy because it was the first NFL game ever to be forced, by rule, into overtime, and the first NFL title game whose outcome would be determined in sudden-death play.

For the record, prior to the 1974 regular season, league games that ended with the score knotted after four quarters were declared ties. In the 1930s, a rule regulating playoff games was drawn up requiring ties to be broken in overtime play.

The Colts' classic win (or, perhaps, not so classic—the game saw eight fumbles and eight sacks) featured two of the most meaningful scoring drives ever. They were witnessed by a sellout crowd in venerable Yankee Stadium and by an estimated 45 million more over national television, marking the largest NFL audience ever. Needing a field goal to tie the contest at 17, the Colts took possession of the football on their own 14-yard line with just 1:56 to go.

Unitas, unfazed, hit Lenny Moore for 11 yards, then hooked up with Berry three times in a row, good for 62 total yards. Moments later, with just seven seconds left in regulation, Steve Myhra, who had earlier missed two field goals, tied things up with a 20-yard field goal. The Colts had consummated a do-or-die 73-yard march.

Looking back on the drive, Berry said, "When we got in the huddle, I looked down the field. The goal posts looked like they were in Baltimore." He went on:

> It ended up being the biggest game of our career, our first championship. Some time later it soaked in on me that, in the two-minute drive to tie that game, John came to me three times in a row, which was very unusual in that situation. And I said, "Explain why you came to me three times in a row." He said, "Oh, I figured you'd catch it."
>
> He kinda had a dry sense of humor, but, as I started to understand football players more and what makes athletes tick, what you were looking at here was an instinctive player doing what he felt like would succeed. I'm not really sure it was a thinking process as much as it was him knowing what to do. Why he'd come to me three times in a row—that just never happens.
>
> You couldn't help but kind of shake your head and say, "Good grief, I've never seen anything like that." Well, nobody else had either. We certainly hadn't.

After the Giants failed to score in overtime, the legendary quarterback once more worked his "Unitas Magic," carving up the Giants' defense while methodically moving the ball 80 yards in 13 plays. He began by quickly cashing in on two first downs. Later, on a third-and-15, he hit Berry for 21 yards; then, always astute, he called an audible that unleashed Alan Ameche, who rambled for 23 yards.

The next key play, another that surprised nearly everyone, was a six-yard pass to another Pennsylvania native, Jim Mutscheller out of Beaver Falls High School. He snagged the ball, but accidentally fell one yard shy of the goal line. When he returned to the huddle, Unitas, true to character, did not deride him. Instead, keeping the moment light, he joked, "Jim, I tried to make you a hero." Moments later came the famous one-yard plunge off right tackle by Ameche (a distant relative of movie actor Don Ameche) to give Baltimore a 23–17 decision.

Later, when asked why the Colts didn't just go for a field goal after getting the ball to within a yard from the goal line, Unitas said, "No offense, but I couldn't trust Myhra. We had to score." The clear inference was that Unitas, with total conviction, *did* believe in *his* offense.

He was convinced the Giants would key on Lenny Moore, who once scored in a record 18 consecutive games. He also believed that, if he called Ameche's number, Moore could get the job done with a vital block. He often seemed to sense just the right play to call, and this time that knack paid off with an NFL title.

At the start of the game-winning drive, Unitas had told teammates, "We've got 80 yards to go and two minutes to do it in. We're going to see what stuff we're made of." After he proved he had the right stuff, Sid Gillman, a quarterback who, quite naturally, admired Unitas, said, "I don't know what he uses for blood, but I guarantee you it isn't warm. It's ice-cold."

Moore said the Colts "knew when that thing went into overtime, what we could do. We felt that way against *any* of the other teams, even the teams that we lost to. My thing was to listen to Johnny U.—everything that Johnny U. said—and shut your mind off to any of the other voices that are coming across the line trying to intimidate you. If you listen to Johnny everything will be OK."

Marchetti observed, "John wasn't afraid of hard work and he wasn't afraid to take chances. If you check back on that championship game of 1958, we're down practically in the end zone and he throws a pass. How many quarterbacks would have enough guts to do that—to throw to Mutscheller? But when they asked John about it, John just said, 'You're not taking a chance if you know what you're doing.'"

That pass play was also a prime example of something Moore said:

Johnny ran the huddle. If they sent something in from the bench, and he didn't like it, he wouldn't call it. Usually if something came in from the bench, that's something you're supposed to immediately call. If Johnny didn't like it, he'd say, "Hell, that damn thing won't work," and he would go on and call whatever he wanted to call. And when he came off the field, the coach [might say], "John, why didn't you call my play?" He'd say, "Hey, I'm here—I can see what's happening." No, Johnny was completely in charge. He took care of business at quarterback.

Ziemann believes Unitas pioneered the types of things quarterbacks would do ages later, such as, say, Peyton Manning calling the play at the line of scrimmage. Berry agreed: "There's no question about it. The circumstances that existed were because of Weeb Ewbank who had enough instinctive sense to let John Unitas call the plays."

In fact, Unitas called audibles and ran the two-minute drill to perfection, decades before the birth of men such as Manning.

Mike Ditka takes Unitas's pioneer status further. "The advent of the forward pass being *really* a weapon was with Johnny Unitas more than anybody."

Colts defensive back Andy Nelson said, "Unitas was a private guy and a cool customer. Nothing excited him. I walked off the field after that [1958 title] game and he wasn't turning back flips or jumping up and down. His eyes were focused straight ahead. Like it was just another game. I thought, 'This man just played the greatest game of his life, and it's like another game to him.' He just casually walked off. He took it all in stride even with reporters buzzing around him."

Unitas's son Joe said his father told him the reason he simply turned and walked off the field was self-evident: "The game was over." Joe observed, "He was a very matter-of-fact person. Black and white—you're right or you're wrong. I probably should have expected that."

Nelson continued: "When we got to the airport, there were 30,000 people waiting for us, [some climbed] on top of the team bus. I rode home with him that night, and he never said two words. I got out of the car and he said, 'I'll see you tomorrow,' and that was it." It was as if they were two buddies leaving a factory after putting in an eight-hour shift. Unitas then went home, had a sandwich and a beer, and went to bed.

Again, such behavior displayed the same nonchalance he had exhibited at the moment of Ameche's touchdown. Marchetti's memory of the end of the game: "If you see the film and you watch John closely, he'll hand the ball off and he'll watch Ameche go in for the score to win the game. And, as casually as he could do it, he started walking off the field. He didn't run, he didn't jump, he didn't point to God up in the sky. He didn't do any of that—just handed the ball off and when Ameche went across, he just walked right off the field very, very slowly and casually. Another day at the office."

Leonard Unitas once ran into one of the refs from the 1958 title game. "He told me that, whenever the Colts had the ball and were [driving] for the field goal, John asked how much time he had left. The ref said 58 seconds and John said, 'Well, that's plenty of time.' The ref said he was thinking, 'Man, he's a smart ass,' but then he said John made a believer out of him."

Unitas won a Corvette for his 26-of-40, 349-yards thrown performance—a new record for a title game, breaking the mark set by Sammy Baugh in 1937. Unitas had deftly engineered the game-winning drive using, as usual, a desire to win that burned with klieg-light intensity. Kudos and universal recognition followed.

Not that he craved such things. Leonard said that, for his brother, "It was all about winning games—it wasn't money, it wasn't fame. He always loved football."

Ed Sullivan wanted Unitas to make a brief appearance in the audience of his television show. Unitas refused the easy $500 paycheck for the cameo shot, preferring to fly home with the team and then quickly return to his family.

His son Chad noted, "He wasn't a flashy person—I mean, for the MVP he won a 1958 Corvette. Well, he traded that in for a station wagon because he had a couple of kids at the time and his thing was, 'What the hell am I going to do with this car?' None of the fame and the extra stuff that comes with it, that wasn't real important to him."

Writer Robert Smith stated Unitas, who did pocket $4,718.77 for winning the championship, quickly became regarded as the best football player alive by the "cool, indomitable and disciplined way he had just won 'the greatest football game ever played.'"

Another writer said that the name *Unitas* "suggests a hero out of the *Chip Hilton* series for young readers: Johnny Unitas. Johnny Unite Us. The hero who never fails to lead his team to victory in the final seconds. The unflappable Unitas did precisely that many times, most famously on December 28, 1958." It's true that, just like Unitas himself, that championship game will never be forgotten.

The 1959 repeat title, coming on the heels of a 9–3 season, reinforced public opinion about Unitas, the season's MVP, and the Colts. That season was one of his best ever. Over the 12-game schedule, he threw the ball 378 times and hit his man 190 times for 2,899 yards and an astonishing 32 touchdowns against 14 interceptions. Previously no man had ever achieved the 30-touchdown plateau; over a 12-game schedule, he remains the *only* quarterback with 30+ touchdown strikes. His 1959 passer rating was 92.0, and 8.7 percent of his passes found the end zone, which is still 22nd on the all-time list.

The championship game, again versus the Giants, wound up with the Colts eventually cruising to a 31–16 win in Baltimore's Memorial Stadium. Nelson stated:

> We just put together a good run. We had some great players: Lenny Moore, Gino Marchetti, and all. You get that winning attitude, and we kept it through most of the season, and we wind up playing the Giants again.
>
> It wasn't easy for a half. I made the key play. I intercepted a pass and ran it back to the nine yard line. It was pretty close up until then. Then when Johnny hit Jerry Richardson for a [fourth quarter] touchdown, we opened it up.

Prior to that, Unitas had thrown a 60-yard score to Moore, and he scampered for a short touchdown as well.

Berry said, "John hit Lenny Moore on a long one. What the Giants were doing was overloading the defense on me. And Moore was sitting over there in one on one, and John went to work with him. And we had Ameche [giving us] a real solid running game. If they overloaded on me, John had sense enough to go to Moore and Mutscheller, which he did, and the defense did their normal thing."

Two key third-down conversions stand out. Once needing 17 yards, Unitas threw for 29; another time the Colts were a distant 21 yards away from the first-down stick, and he launched a pass for 31. Unitas earned another Corvette as the game's best player, and he again got rid of it.

The following four seasons weren't so kind to the Colts. In 1960 they inexplicably faltered (6–6), and then went 8–6, 7–7, and, in their first season under Don Shula, 8–6. They had plummeted from lofty heights to becoming not much better than a break-even club. Unitas, for the most part, though, remained superb. In 1960, he threw for 3,099 yards and 25 TDs, while leading the NFL in five major categories. In both 1961 and 1962, he fell just short of 3,000 yards—by a combined total of 43 yards. In 1963, he fired the ball for a personal high 3,481 yards, marking the first of two seasons in which he'd top the 3,400 plateau. He remains the only man to enter the 3,000-yard stratum over a 12-game season.

A return to good times came in 1964 when Unitas, the NFL's MVP, averaged 9.3 yards gained per pass attempt. That figure was then the 5th best ever and still ranks 13th best. Plus, he averaged 17.9 yards per completion that season, which is still the 11th best average ever.

The Colts coasted to a 12–2 record to win the West Division. Unfortunately, the Cleveland Browns blanked them, scoring all of their 27 points in the second half.

Baltimore was again atop their division in 1965 (tied with Green Bay at 10–3–1), but entered postseason play with running back Tom Matte forced into quarterback duties. Unitas, injured, was out since last playing on December 5. Three weeks later, Green Bay defeated the Colts, 13–10, for the right to advance to the playoffs. This time it was the Colts who experienced the agony of a loss in overtime.

In 1967 the Rams and Colts tied for their division leadership, sharing the best record in the league, 11–1–2. Their only loss was in the season's final game to Los Angeles. However, due to the rules of the day, the Colts, despite being tied with the Rams, did not qualify for postseason play. That didn't stop voters from giving Unitas his third MVP trophy.

The Colts were a juggernaut (13–1) in 1968, but Unitas was out of the picture for the most part, throwing just 32 passes on the regular season. In the final preseason game, Unitas "crippled his elbow," and he did not start a game all season long. Remarkably, his backup, the 34-year-old journeyman Earl Morrall took over, and he copped the league's MVP award as he led Baltimore into Super Bowl III.

Of course, the defeat against the underdog Jets (discussed in more detail in Namath's chapter) shocked most of the football world.

Colts safety Rick Volk said of the loss, "I think Joe Namath always felt that, when John came in the game, they were in trouble; and we did get a touchdown. You got to go along with the coach's decision, and John's arm had been hurt that year and Earl had played real well, but Earl was not effective that much in that game. People have said that if Shula had put him in earlier, maybe it would have been a different story."

When Unitas did enter the game, Volk felt the Colts had a chance to roar back: "I knew we had a shot, but we as the defensive unit weren't able to stop the Jets from getting first downs, and they were able to control the ball. We just weren't able to execute. Namath sort of picked us apart, moving it down the field. It was just one of those games when I realized [later] that anything can happen in a football game. And even if you're 17-point favorites, in a Super Bowl game you can still get beat if somebody happens to make some key plays and eliminate mistakes—they have a better chance of winning."

Another factor is that Jets coach Weeb Ewbank was not too far removed from having coached the Colts. Volk said, "He knew all the personnel here. He knew everybody's weakness."

The Colts were a dynastic team. From December 18, 1966, until the loss in Super Bowl III, they were virtually invincible, playing 30 games and losing just twice.

Unitas got a championship ring two seasons later when his Colts (11–2–1) knocked off the Dallas Cowboys in Super Bowl V. Unitas, no longer sporting a crew cut, may have been 37 years old, but he was proficient enough to win 10 of his starts. He led the NFL in a category for the last time, manufacturing three fourth-quarter comebacks, good for the seventh time he led or tied for the lead in that department. In the Super Bowl, Earl Morrall replaced the injured Unitas near halftime, but not before Unitas had completed three passes, one a 75-yard TD to John Mackey.

Rick Volk suggested one reason for this win: "We went down with a little different attitude in Super Bowl V. Number one, the wives weren't staying with us, where they were the week for Super Bowl III—I remember we just were not really focused on why we really were there, and I think were too confident. We were more or less worried about what we were going to do during the day and evening than we were about getting prepared to play the Jets."

In the 1971 season, at the age of 38, Unitas and the Colts could have made it to another Super Bowl if they had been able to get by the Miami Dolphins in the AFC title game, but it wasn't to be. Still, Unitas and Morrall had helped take the Colts to a fine 10–4 regular season record.

Unitas married Sandy shortly before his final season with the Colts in 1972. When asked what attracted her to Johnny in the first place, she replied:

I don't think anything attracted me to him. I was an airline stewardess, and I had a part time job in promotional work, and I didn't even know who he was until a year before [she formally met him]. I was working a Jackie Gleason golf tournament in Miami, working the V.I.P. gate, and a driver came up without the right credentials. I said, "I'm sorry, you can't go through." He said, "Do you know who this is in the back seat?" I looked back there and said, "No. I don't know who he is." He said, "I think you better go see your supervisor. This is John Unitas."

Still unimpressed, she persisted: "I don't know who John Unitas is." That was the first time she laid eyes upon her future husband.

A year later, still doing promotional work while still working as a stewardess out of Florida, she was assigned to work the Johnny Unitas Football Game in Baltimore around Christmas. There, she actually met Unitas, but even then, she recounted, "There wasn't any attraction there at all. In fact, I thought he looked really old. His hair was growing out at the time, and it was spiked all over his head—it looked goofy." His regular barber who worked on his crew cut was no longer available so Unitas had begun to let it grow out. "He never went back to the crew cut after that," said Sandy. He did, however, eventually begin to grow on Sandy, and they later fell in love.

When Unitas bowed out after spending 1973 with the San Diego Chargers he "was broken down at forty, barely able to reach up and drag a pocket comb through his [hair]. . . . Waiting for the pass rush, he said, felt like, 'Okay, Buick, run me down.'" He fully realized it was time to call it quits. His body had paid the cost for the glory of playing and excelling in a smash-mouth game for so long. Surprisingly, he played the only game of his career in his hometown of Pittsburgh in his last NFL start and the next-to-last game of his career. He separated his shoulder in his final game ever on November 4. That was it, an inglorious way to bow out for a legend.

Unitas's talent and style have been evaluated ad infinitum. For example, sportswriter Bob Carroll described Unitas as "an arrogant gambler who held the outcome of [the game] in the palm of his hand." Unitas himself told writers that, when it came to running his team, "it's gamble or die. I'm no conservative."

Defensive back Johnny Sample, who played with and against Unitas, noted that Unitas "wasn't graceful or nifty, he was actually kind of awkward, but he had a helluva arm, strong. He was a daring passer, and he used surprise as a weapon. . . . he'd do the unexpected."

Marchetti said, "Most of all, I think, John should be known more for his leadership, for his attitude towards the game, and the hours that he put in studying during the week of the game. It's not like now, they have coordinators and everything that call the plays. When John was the quarterback in those days, they had to know the offensive plans, they had to know what you do on third-and-two, third-and-three, and that type of thing. They had to study. During the season, I don't think they had as much fun because they had to work too hard to study the plays and call their own plays. Weeb might have called five or six plays a game or whatever, but nowadays I don't know how many they call."

Berry once stated, "John was a field general. He had this rare ability to make the game conform to his will. He controlled the tempo, decided the tactics. He was a chess master who played the game several moves ahead of everyone else."

The analogy of a quarterback to a master chess player, seeing everything on the board and staying multiple moves ahead of the opponent is appropriate. Havrilak stated: "In those days, quarterbacks called their own plays. So John would deliberately run plays to set things up, maybe a quarter or two ahead of time, in his mind. He would run certain pass patterns continuously with a receiver, then suddenly call a different pass pattern, off the same formation against the same defenses so the defensive back would think the play was going one way when, actually, John was just setting him up to do something else." He lured unwary defensive backs in, suckered them, many a time.

Unitas was shrewd. Tom Matte said:

He would talk to us during the game, "All right, now listen—I want to be able to send the slant end, take off sideline [a play that often utilized Jimmy Orr]. Set that up. Make them think you're going deep, and I'll lead you out to the sideline." Every plan was designed. John was a mathematician as far as I was concerned. He knew what he wanted to do, he wanted to set it up, and when he did set up, it worked. That's what made him one of the greatest quarterbacks ever to play the game.

Unitas possessed a blend of instinct and, said Matte, "football intelligence up the ying-yang."

Georgia head coach Vince Dooley drew a comparison between Unitas and Fran Tarkenton, whom he watched "beat Auburn in a championship game on a fourth down play which he designed that scored the winning touchdown with 30 seconds left." He said that the smart quarterbacks like

Unitas improvised on the spot. "The guys that are the real leaders, the take-charge type quarterbacks, they'll do that—they have this confidence."

Colts head coach Weeb Ewbank, the first coach to win championships in the NFL (with Unitas) and the AFL (with Namath), chipped in: "Unitas was excellent at reading defenses, but he was also the first to master the art of 'looking off'—looking at one side of the field or even faking a throw to make the defense flinch and then suddenly throwing the ball elsewhere. The great quarterbacks always complete the 'one-on-ones.' When a guy was wide open, John never missed him, he always hit him."

From practice sessions, Nelson knew firsthand that "Unitas was different from some of the other quarterbacks in that he looked off his receiver. He didn't 'birddog' the receiver. That's when a receiver is out there running a pattern, and the quarterback watches him all the way down. That makes it easy for a defensive back. John looked off; he looked one way, and if a defensive back was reading his eyes, John's throwing him off. Then he comes back to the other side. A lot of quarterbacks didn't do that, and that was one of his strengths."

Lucci agreed: "Unitas had a great feel of the game, and of the field, and he did look you off a lot. I mean, he'd go and come back to a receiver, or he'd look one way and then come back to where he intended to go all along. He had a great ability to do that."

Unitas once verified (as if it needed verification) his field general/chess master status. "Our coach [Ewbank] never called the plays. He turned the game plan over to me." He related how Colts personnel in the press box would ask him what information he wanted, and all he cared to learn was if his opponent had any tendencies regarding blitzing with their linebackers. "Otherwise," he instructed them, "just sit there and enjoy the game."

In 1960, Unitas was suffering from a fractured vertebra in his back, and all he managed to do was lead the NFL in passes attempted and completed, yards through the air, and touchdowns thrown. Writer Bob Carroll credited, in part, Unitas's ability to coolly hold onto "the football under a rush until the last possible split second, allowing his receivers to break loose of coverage." Unitas did that in spite of the risk of being inundated and punished by the rush of defenders—and despite his many injuries over the years, including torn arm tendons and knee cartilage, broken fingers, and myriad so-called minor injuries.

Unlike some quarterbacks who get happy feet and get sacked or throw balls away prematurely, Unitas fearlessly hung in there, often taking terrible licks from massive linemen and rampaging linebackers as the price for throwing a pass at the last second possible.

Carroll, who saw Unitas as "a hard-nose winner," said some observers believed he held on to the ball so long as a symbolic gesture, displaying "his disdain for frustrated pass rushers." Perhaps, though, it was more a case of showing his confidence and toughness: he was quite willing to take a hit if it meant helping his Colts win.

He took the Colts to the 1958 title despite playing with a punctured lung and broken ribs. In 1960 he played the full schedule with a broken vertebra. One writer called him "as tough as tungsten, just like his hometown," and elaborated on his physical woes while tossing in a few more of Unitas's injuries and health issues: a ruptured Achilles in his right foot, shoulder contusions, knee surgeries, and the ripped tendon in his throwing arm, which was "almost off the bone."

Bimbo Cecconi, a standout quarterback at Pitt, remembers Unitas, the first quarterback ever to top 40,000 yards passing, as an "old blood and guts" quarterback who repeatedly got racked up, yet came back for more pain, but with many wins to offset the agony. "He ended up with fingers that he couldn't even move. He would write his autograph by sticking the pen between his fingers propping the pen up." His toughness, said Cecconi, was simply, "like Blanda, old school."

Playing football led to Unitas going through at least 12 fairly major surgeries. Chad Unitas said:

> I've never seen anybody with a stronger threshold for pain than what he had. I've watched him go through a bunch of different surgeries and his first heart attack and never saw him complain about anything. He was a very tough man. . . .
>
> I played golf with him, and he had no strength in his right hand—the muscle in his hand was dead, he couldn't rotate his thumb, he didn't have feeling in the tips of his fingers in his right hand, he couldn't hold a cup of coffee in his right hand or tie his shoes or undo his belt or zip his zipper, but, again, he never complained and he was still out there playing golf all the time. He had a glove that he wore on the right hand, he'd put his hand in there, and he had a Velcro strip that came around and he Velcroed his hand onto the golf club just so he could hold on to it.

Many times Unitas seemed impervious to injury. He certainly was resilient: after sustaining a serious injury in 1965, he threw for 22 touchdowns and amassed 2,748 yards passing in 1966, and then 3,428 yards in 1967 when he led the NFL by completing 58.5 percent of his passes.

Unitas revealed that one season, "The Bears had a bounty on me for $500. . . . One of the players told me. They said, 'Anybody that knocks him out of the ball game gets an extra $500.' I never worried about that. A quarterback who's looking at the rush instead of his receivers shouldn't be playing in the NFL."

Former New York Giants general manager Ernie Accorsi said, "What made him the greatest quarterback of all time wasn't his arm or his size, it was what was inside his stomach."

Unitas—often battered by vicious defenses of the day, who were unleashed by rules that permitted figurative head-hunting and by unwritten rules that allowed literal bounty hunting of quarterbacks—simply got the job done.

Jim Houston was a star linebacker for the Cleveland Browns from 1960 through 1972. Over that span, he played against Unitas many times. "He was always delivering," Houston said, remembering what made Unitas special, "and you knew you were going to have a real hard job of beating him. You had to consider whatever the plays were that the Colts tended to run and how much they hurt the defenders. In the Browns' case, we always were looking for the right angle to take against him—considering what they did on first down, the second down, the third down. I had to make sure I covered the guys that he was trying to throw to. It just depended on what the film showed and our study, our preparation for the game."

The key was how they would react to Unitas, as Houston fully realized that failure to do so meant Unitas would beat them. The bottom line, though, was simple: "He was hard to contain."

While Unitas certainly didn't have the physique of a decathlon Olympian, Houston said that was immaterial, as Unitas not only *was* quite athletic, but also came through time after time. "He knew what was going to take place on the field. You knew you had to play extra hard on the people he was trying to reach or he'd burn you and you'd lose the game."

Sam Havrilak analyzed Unitas's effectiveness: "By the time I got there [with the Colts], he had had some arm trouble the year before [in 1968] when he didn't play all year. Morrall played all year. So his arm wasn't as strong as it had been when he was younger, but he was so good and he could read defenses so well that, by the time you came out of your break, the ball was already there. It was a matter of timing—he didn't have to throw it hard when you knew where the receiver was going to be. Not like, for example, Namath whose arm was so strong that he could wait until the receiver made the break and then rifle the ball in there. The same thing with Bert Jones—their arms were so strong that they could do that. But with John, at that stage in his career, he couldn't do that. But the ball was always there when you came out of the break."

NFL kicker Fred Cox called Unitas the "prototype for all of them. It was a different type of game when he was playing. He just had a great arm and, in a lot of ways, he was totally different than the quarterbacks [of today] because when he was playing the quarterback didn't move around. He was a drop-back passer—and you stayed there in the pocket. It's quite obvious that his accuracy and his arm strength were just phenomenal."

Ultimately, said Houston, although all six of the Hall of Fame quarterbacks from the Pittsburgh area "were super athletes—good in any situation, Unitas [is my pick] as the best."

Andy Nelson commented: "He threw a pretty hard ball, but he could soften it up sometimes when he had a guy in the open, and sometimes he had to lob it for a swing pass out of the backfield—he'd let a running back run under it, but he drilled it [usually] like when a defensive back was close to the receiver—he could rifle it so the defensive back couldn't recover. Those sideline passes to Raymond Berry were drilled. He had a strong arm."

His style was definitely unique. Year after year, Unitas methodically took snap after snap after snap from his center and let his feet, adorned in his trademark black, high-top football shoes, drop him back into the pocket with almost mincing, chop-chop steps. Then, protected in that pocket of teammates, he dismantled defenses from coast to coast.

Havrilak said: "He was very, very calm. I know because we went by jersey numbers in the locker room so Earl Morrall was 15, I was 17, and John was 19, so I lockered between those guys for two or three years. After he had his arm massaged before the game, John would often go into the training room and sleep for about 30 or 40 minutes."

Volk concurred: "John didn't go out and do a Ray Lewis and get everybody all fired up, that kind of thing. He was just a straightforward person—he was all business—and he told it like it was, 'Let's get ready and go out and play. Let's go.' But those are the kinds of guys that you look up to because they've been through the war, so to speak."

Paige Unitas remarked that her mother said Unitas's calm demeanor would make her nervous when he "threw the ball at the end of the game, and he's off the field before the guy's even caught it. He told her, 'My job was done. I'm not going to catch it.'"

Havrilak told a similar tale. "We played a game down in Houston in 1970, and we won it in the last few seconds when John threw a touchdown pass to Roy Jefferson in the corner of the end zone. When you saw the films of the game, after he threw the pass, John just started running off the field. The reporters asked him, 'Why didn't you wait to see if he caught the ball,' And John said, 'I threw it right where he should have been, and if he didn't catch it, then we lost the game, and I couldn't do anything else.'"

Cecconi also admired Unitas's composure. "When things were going tough, he was just perfect—his capabilities of getting the ball in there, scoring touchdowns, and being a leader. And he wasn't fancy, he wasn't fast, he wasn't big, but Johnny Unitas could do it all."

Unitas's expression seldom changed—win or lose. Ziemann recalled a story about Dick Butkus taunting Unitas with ominous words like, "I'm going to tear your face off. I'm going to kill you." Unitas wouldn't even glance his way. Moments later he'd complete a pass for, say, a 10-yard pickup. Butkus spewed more venom, "I'm going to gouge your eyes out and break your legs." Twenty-yard completion. Ziemann picked up the story, "Finally, after Butkus said, 'I'm going to tear your head off. There won't be nothing left of you except a pulp.' Touchdown. Butkus said Unitas then would do the ultimate act. 'He'd walk away, look back at me with that crooked Lithuanian grin. That's when I *really* wanted to kill him.' The night Butkus concluded that story at a banquet. Unitas just looked at him and grinned. Butkus shouted, 'See! Look at that grin. Look at that grin.'"

Unitas was, in today's vernacular, old school—from his signature crew cut he had seemingly forever, to the high-top shoes he preferred, his brother says, since high school, to his distinctive staccato steps as he dropped back to pass. If he threw a game-winning touchdown or was picked off due to a poor pass, his stoical reaction was the same. Carroll noted, "If you can imagine Johnny U. leering at a TV camera with his index finger stabbing a 'number one,' you can conceive the Washington Monument doing a hula."

Praise for Johnny U. is universal. Here was a man who, arguably, more than anyone else, deserved to be thought of as Johnny Football. One of his admirable traits was, observed Carroll, "his ability to get better when things got tougher. No quarterback could bring a team back like Unitas, no one could use the clock better, no one could hit the pass that *had* to be made as often."

Dooley said, "Unitas was just a classic drop-back passer, more so than any that I remember. He had incredibly disciplined receivers with him. He was not [like] the athletes that we see today in, say, the San Francisco quarterback [Colin Kaepernick]. But, at the same time, he excelled at two aspects of the game: (1) what he did so well in the drop back, and (2) the leadership qualities that he had—always the hardest thing to measure."

Carroll noted that there was a cornucopia of great quarterbacks in the 1960s, with men such as Bart Starr, Sonny Jurgensen, Don Meredith, John Brodie, and Tarkenton, "But the crème de la crème was Johnny U. If he wasn't the best pure passer in the league (and he was close), he was certainly the most effective."

Unitas helped others get better, too, but he wouldn't force lessons upon them. Sam Havrilak, whom Unitas called "the greatest utility man I ever worked with," said: "Any time I asked John after practice to stay and work on something, he would always do it, but he wouldn't do it on his own. You'd have to ask him to do it, but if you did, he'd be happy to stay out there as long as you wanted to stay."

Sometimes the help Unitas provided was indirect. Nelson said that practicing against Unitas "made us better because we were practicing against the best."

Volk said going against Unitas in practice was a blessing. "He prepared his offensive and also our defensive team. I always said that if you could play and do well in our practices, we would have an advantage when we went out and played other teams just because we're playing every day against Johnny U. and some of the talented receivers that he had."

Paige Unitas said: "He wasn't ever demanding. He was never scary— 'You have to do what I say or I'll kill you.' No, you respected him. His teammates loved him, respected him, and he was so good to everybody on the field. If you didn't do something right, he'd give you another chance. He wanted you to succeed. If you messed up again, get out of here." The team was too important for Unitas to put with up those who would hurt it, but for the most part the team was highly professional and meshed beautifully with him.

John Mackey often told the story about dropping what should have been a routine catch. As boos cascaded down, he dreaded going back to the huddle, fearing banishment to the sidelines. "I think he was a rookie that year," Paige said. "He goes back and my dad called the same play, and he looked him right in the eyes and said, 'Silence the crowd.'" Paige said Mackey did just that. "I think he scored [on the next play]. Later Mackey told Paige, "That's the way your dad said, 'I believe in you. It's OK that you messed up, but let's fix it.'"

That is not to say there were never circumstances when Unitas would resist chastising someone who needed a kick in the butt. Nelson said: "I never saw him do that unless he was a rookie, never a veteran. It depended on the situation, like if someone wasn't trying hard or wasn't working at his craft, John might step in there and say something. He wasn't a hollering or a rah-rah guy."

Havrilak added: "When John was in the huddle, he was in command. You didn't speak unless he asked you a question. He'd ask what you had if you were a receiver as far as what you could get open on. He didn't tolerate mental mistakes. If anybody made enough mental mistakes, he'd tell them to get out of the game and get somebody else in that can do it." One teammate called the Colts' huddle "Unitas's cathedral."

Tom Matte reflected: "John was probably the coolest guy, never got upset. He got back in the huddle and never pointed any fingers at anybody for making a blown assignment or something like that, but you walk in the huddle and he'd bend over and he'd sort of talk out of the side of his mouth, 'Hey, Matte. Do you want to play quarterback again today?' I'd say, 'No, John.' He'd say, 'Then you'd better block.' Or if a receiver dropped a pass, the first thing you'd say, 'I'm sorry, John.' He'd say, 'Catch the ball. Look it into your hands.' Subtle stuff. No yelling, no screaming."

Volk stated, "A lot of the guys on our team felt we had a seven-point advantage before we went onto the field every game because of John. If we were behind by three, four, or seven, we always had confidence that

John knew what he was doing, and he would end up winning the game for us because he just had that ability to make big plays." Just as he did in 1958 with his patented two-minute drill.

However, as Ziemann praised, "John never took credit for a win, but he accepted the blame for losses."

Berry said that one of the most interesting characteristics of Unitas that "comes to my mind is his absolute focus on football. He was single-minded in his approach to the game. He had three interests: one was football, the second was football, and the third was football. The number two [characteristic] that comes to my mind is his toughness and his competitive spirit—he was beyond intimidation. He was the toughest guy on the football team, and he would have made one helluva linebacker. With that temperament, if he had the linebacker physical stuff, he would have been a Hall of Famer."

Former NFL scout Dick Bestwick singled out Unitas as the best ever from the Pittsburgh area. "I start with Unitas. He's a perfect example of the great quarterbacks we've had in Western Pennsylvania. It would be hard for anybody to do much more than him, but I certainly wouldn't be afraid to go to war with Marino or Kelly or Montana—how can you be much better than him?"

Bestwick gives the edge to Unitas over others because of "the fact that he did it at such a high level for so long. He took the Colts to unbelievable success during his tenure as a quarterback." Further, if Unitas had been transplanted in time and locale and become the 49ers quarterback instead of Montana, Bestwick believes, "He'd have had as much success as anybody they've had there because he just had those kind of skills and leadership qualities."

Colt teammates such as Nelson confirmed that. "He was well respected. He led by example. He worked hard, he played when he was hurt, and he went through some tough times, and the players all looked up to him, but he didn't go around preaching to them. He wasn't that type."

Sandy Unitas said that, unlike many stars, instead of displaying pride over his football feats, "he more or less took it routinely. He knew it was a God-given ability, but he also knew that throughout his years of play, even in high school, he had to work at it—he didn't just take it for granted. He was very focused, and he continuously worked on that ability. I'm sure you've heard stories about him staying after practice with Raymond Berry and throwing passes and throwing passes and throwing passes. Football was very much a part of his life, but it wasn't what he was on this earth for." In short, he was a perfectionist as a player, but not monomaniacal about it.

"He was not, by any means, an obsessive, compulsive type. He was very disciplined," continued Sandy. "If he started a job, he would finish it. He was very laid back, easy going, but when he put his mind to something, he did it. What I learned over the 32 years we were together, if he told you he was going to do something, then he would do it.

"That was so true, even on the morning of the day that he died. He had promised an old friend that he would meet him for breakfast." In the meantime, things had gotten a bit hectic, and Sandy suggested her fatigued husband cancel the meal. "He said, 'No. I told him I'd be there, I'll be there.' That's what he always did no matter how tired he was—he had a commitment, he saw it through." Most often, of course, the commitment was to his family, his team, and his own heart.

What Unitas had to say when he retired reflected his lifelong values and his workmanlike approach to his life. "I came into the league without any fuss. I'd just as soon leave it that way. There's no difference I can see in retiring from pro football or quitting a job at the Pennsy Railroad. I did something I wanted to do and went as far as I could."

By the time Unitas peeled off his No. 19 jersey for the final time, he had cemented his reputation as being not just a great, but also legendary NFL figure. In 2008, writer Allan Maki opined, "No one tougher, no one smarter, no one more courageous has ever played the position. Johnny Unitas defied eras."

Ziemann said Unitas figuratively invented the modern quarterback: "John created the modern quarterback—he was the foundation. He and the Colts invented the two-minute drill, and all of the stuff they were doing, they're still doing today. All of his records may be broken someday, but he will always be the Babe Ruth of pro football."

Unitas died at the age of 69 while riding an exercise bike on September 11, 2002, exactly one year after 9/11. Former teammate Jim Parker wept upon hearing the news and commented, "It was the first time that I wasn't there to protect him."

The Sunday after Unitas died, Peyton Manning expressed his desire to wear black high-tops to honor Unitas, but the league prohibited him from doing so. He even suggested every player in the NFL should have worn such shoes.

His legend definitely lives on. When his son Joe became a father in 2005, he named him Colten John Unitas, figuring his son's name would eventually be shortened by friends to Colt.

John Mackey was once asked what it was like playing with Unitas. His terse reply: "It's like being in the huddle with God."

JOE NAMATH

4 "No Brag. Just Fact"

SELECT LIFETIME FACTS, statistics, and records of note: Namath was AFL Rookie of the Year in 1965, and he soared from there. Twenty years later, he was inducted into the Pro Football Hall of Fame. Along the way, he led his league in passing and yards passing three times, in completions and total offense twice, and most touchdowns passing once. One little-known stat reveals how Namath loved to go deep: his 14.7 yards for each of his career completions is still, through the 2016 season, the 11th best average ever. He was also the AFL MVP in 1968 and was named to five Pro Bowl teams.

• • •

Writers have worn out many a thesauri seeking labels and descriptions of Joe Namath—from nouns like *iconoclast, rebel,* and *hedonist,* to terse adjectives such as *arrogant, brash,* and *flamboyant.* They have called him a star, but also an antihero who came along at just the right time during the tumultuous 1960s. He wore flashy clothes, such as white spikes and a full-length mink coat during his playing days; at the age of 70, he donned a full-length fur coat on Groundhog Day in 2014, when he tossed the ceremonial coin prior to Super Bowl XLVIII. And he frequently gleamed his crooked little smile, charming everyone except members of the conservative establishment. Descriptions were really unnecessary, since everybody knew who and what he was.

As a side note, two days after Super Bowl XLVIII, an editorial cartoon in the *Beaver County Times* poked fun at Namath's sartorial ways. In the cartoon, a man watching the game on TV says, "Six more weeks of winter. Joe Namath's coat just saw his shadow."

So what exactly goes into the making of such a man? One factor that impacted a young Joe Namath and his four older siblings was their parents' divorce. A second key factor was his family's socioeconomic status: growing up in the steel town of Beaver Falls, he never had much money.

Joe was in sixth grade when his parents split up, and he grew up not with his steelworker father, but with his mother. Namath's father, John, worked in a local mill for 51 years, a job that contributed to his breathing problems. His mother, Rose (née Juhasz), worked at a five-and-dime store, struggling to support her family.

His parents' divorce scarred him, and the trauma never fully left his psyche, cropping up again when his wife left him many years later. A sense of lasting stability must have seemed impossible for Namath.

One valuable lesson Joe learned from his father early in life involved the importance of having a wise goal. Joe recounted: "I don't recall him ever telling me that I shouldn't work in the steel mill, but he did walk me through the mill when I was about 11 years old and I'll tell you something, it scared me. It's like 120 degrees by the furnaces—ugly stuff, man. I swore at that time to myself, 'Oh, man, I am not going to come in here.'"

Soon, Joe did bring home some money, but not in a blue-collar fashion. Dan Jenkins wrote, "He shot pool, he shined shoes, he ran messages for bookies, he hustled; he got by." Once Namath commented, "Where I come from, ain't nobody gonna hustle *me.*"

Joe's sister Rita said that when he was young she sometimes thought of him as "a pain in the ass." He was quite capable of occasionally getting into typical teenage mischief; he was also charming enough to glibly work his way out of trouble. Many years later, esteemed writer Dave Anderson would call Namath an "attractive wiseguy."

One time Namath and Linwood Alford, perhaps Joe's closest friend (who just happened to be African American—Namath was said to have been figuratively color blind), pushed their impish ways too far. They decided to suspend themselves from a railroad trestle. Alford related: "We were laughing. We held on till the train went by, then we climbed back up. Joe's father gave us some whupping that day, boy."

Another close friend, Wibby Glover, said one time he and Namath got into some typical teen mischief. "We were arrested for trying to do some vandalism." The police took him to the station; but when the police chief heard what was going on, he told Glover to get Joe out of there because he had a game the next day.

Other facets of Namath, dating back to his youth, include his generosity, thoughtfulness, and loyalty. Betsy McGurgan of Beaver Falls said, "Joe has always been true to his friends."

Ken Thomas, one year behind Namath at Beaver Falls High, tells the story of an annual town auction to raise money for a good cause, "In 2012, there was a signed New York Jets [Namath] jersey; the bidding got up to $400, $1,000. It got to a little over $2,000—there were two main bidders at this point—and Joe stood up. He said, 'If you both want one of those shirts, I'll get another one and sign it and I'll get it to you.'" Then, comically alluding to his famous Super Bowl prediction, he said, "And, I guarantee it."

Further, when Colts safety Rick Volk sustained a concussion in Super Bowl III, Namath had flowers sent to Volk's hospital room. No ulterior motive. "It was with good intentions—it wasn't trying to rub it in," said Volk.

As for Namath the athlete, Beaver Falls native Steve Higgins—like Namath, a football player at the University of Alabama—said that, at first, "Joe was like every other kid from Beaver Falls. He went to the Catholic School, St. Mary's. In junior high he went out for the team, but he wasn't a big star, just one of the guys."

Although he loved sports, he got off to a slow start. As a kid playing baseball from Pony League into American Legion ball, Namath was, said Thomas, "relatively small. We called him Little Joe, not to his face though. In ninth grade, junior high, Joe probably wouldn't have started, except the guy who was slated to play quarterback broke his hand. His talent was evident then."

One source lists Namath as 5'9"and just under 100 pounds when he entered high school. Higgins said: "In junior high he *was* small. He barely made the team in high school. His sophomore year he played one play. His junior year he got to play sparingly [behind] Rich Neidbala, who got a scholarship to the University of Miami. In Joe's senior year [the 1960 season], they were one of the greatest teams ever—they were ranked No. 5 in the nation, No. 1 in the state." By then, Namath, an All-State selection, had filled out to 185 pounds.

An all-round high school athlete, who also excelled at golf and pool, Namath's interest in basketball and football hadn't blossomed fully at first, but he did letter three years in baseball, basketball, and football.

Early on, he actually spent some time as a halfback and a defensive back, and he later led his basketball team in dunks. His football coach, Larry Bruno, recalled: "he could throw. . . . We based our whole offense on his ability. All the plays were formulated with him in mind."

Bruno, who felt Namath had the highest football IQ he ever encountered, continued: "You only had to tell Joe something once. He had the right moves. He had the easy motion when he threw the ball."

Teammates marveled at the speed with which the "slight and skinny" Namath threw a football and a baseball, and Bruno sensed there was something special about this kid. "He had a sizzle about him." Bruno saw Namath as a perfectionist, who would "repeat plays in practice till we got it right."

Bruno once said that, if he had to choose just one word to sum up Namath, it would be *confidence*. Years later as a professional, Namath candidly spoke about his self-assuredness. "I'm convinced I'm better than anybody else. I've been convinced of that for quite a while. I haven't seen anything out there that I couldn't do and do well. . . . I get annoyed with myself for doing something wrong. . . . I tell myself, 'You're the best, damn it, do it right.'"

Bruno said that, unlike the image of Namath as a devil-may-care kind of person, "when it came to football and sports, everything he did was serious. People were jealous of him. He had his own style and some people didn't care for it." Bruno recognized Namath as being "cocky and I wanted him to tone it down."

Namath, who seldom toned things down, commented: "To be a leader, you have to make people want to follow you. And nobody wants to follow someone who doesn't know where he's going."

Fred Cox, who feels a quarterback absolutely must ooze confidence, agreed with Namath's assessments, saying, "I think Joe had the biggest ego of all of them [The Six], no question about that. I also think that Joe was so much different from the other guys in that he was much more of a riverboat gambler type of quarterback—he would throw into double coverage more than any guy I ever saw at that stage of the game. Fran Tarkenton and I talked about this a lot, but he got away with it a lot."

Bruno observed that, as a vital side effect of Namath's confidence and ego, "the entire [high school] football team believed whatever play Joe called would work. They would make it work because they knew Joe had confidence in them."

Bruno taught Namath the art of deception; Glover said, "Joe could fake so well into the line, and roll out and then throw a pass, I mean, it was like Mr. Tricky. That was him."

Gimpy later in life, the young and healthy Namath was a fabulous runner. He was shifty and elusive, agile and fast. Gaylon McCollough, a Crimson Tide teammate, later said that trying to take Namath down was "like trying to tackle the wind. He could stop on a dime and throw a jump pass 40 or 50 yards."

When Namath was young, nearly everyone felt baseball was his best sport; in fact, Namath hit .667 for his high school team. Despite coming off a championship football season, Namath didn't appear to be too concerned about playing college football.

A $50,000 offer to play for the Chicago Cubs' organization led to a discussion between his brothers Frank and Bob and his mother. They all knew Joe's main desire was to play baseball; however, when Bob asked their mother for her input, she insisted Joe attend college—and that was that.

Namath received offers from 52 universities, including Notre Dame, but he initially chose Maryland, "because I was stupid enough to think it was down South." His main desire was to avoid bitter winters.

Vince Dooley, who coached for an eon in the Southeastern Conference, said, "He went to Alabama after having fallen short of that required SAT score of the ACC [Atlantic Coast Conference]." A friend of Namath's, Al Hassan, recalled they didn't take studying for the test very seriously, and Joe fell 12 points short of the 750 points he needed on the exam.

He was approached by Alabama because they hadn't signed a quarterback, and the start of the season was looming. Dooley said: "Auburn had dominated all the quarterbacks in the state. Your recruiting was pretty much local, and Alabama just kind of stumbled into Namath. They were looking for a tackle or something and somebody [in Beaver Falls] said, 'Well, we don't have one, but we sure got a quarterback here that just got his test score, and he isn't going to quite make it at Maryland.'"

Plus, the Maryland coach, Tom Nugent, placed a call to Alabama, offering Namath up to them. Nugent figured he'd rather have Namath playing for 'Bama than for a team that he might have to oppose.

From the very start, Namath was, as Jenkins called him, "a happening. He happened first when he was a sophomore passing star who made Alabama coach Bear Bryant change his offense." Alabama went 10–1. "He happened again as a junior [and Alabama posted a 9–2 record], when he proved to be such an away-from-the-field mover that Bryant had to kick him off the team for drinking and carousing before the last two games of the season [causing him to miss playing in the Sugar Bowl]. He happened again when he returned to take Alabama to the 1964 national championship on a gimpy leg."

The 1964 team went 10–1 and was ranked No. 1 by the Associated Press and the United Press International.

His play at Alabama proved what Dooley said: when Namath was on the field, his flamboyance meant nothing. True, here was a kid who was so concerned about his image that, as a high school player, he took to wearing sunglasses frequently, even while posing for team photos for the school yearbook. However, as Dooley noted: "He was all business on the field. He had to be himself off the field, which led to conflicts with Bear Bryant on some occasions, but that's just 'lovable Joe,' I call him. He's the most lovable person that I've ever been around, and fun to be around, charming."

Sportswriter Chuck Finder said: "Alabama was still pretty much a running team under Bryant, but Namath was such a great thrower. It was as if Bryant turned a page and realized [that]. He didn't completely dive into it because he still was a conservative coach at heart." But when Bryant saw a Namath, a Ken Stabler, or a Scott Hunter, he knew what he had to do.

Dooley continued: "When I was a freshman coach at Auburn, freshmen were not eligible. They sign this guy named Namath and we played him, but really didn't know anything about him. But he was just a *total athlete.* He ran the option, he threw the ball, he was just a magnificent athlete at that time—the best kind of athlete that I saw as a quarterback. He was one who could do so many things. Such a natural."

When Gaylon McCollough spotted Namath for the first time, he noticed Namath was jauntily sporting a toothpick in his mouth. When informed that this was the new quarterback in town, McCollough scoffed, saying he would last just a few weeks on campus.

Namath recalled deeper initial animosity. "There were a few upperclassmen at the time that were hard on the kid from Pennsylvania—trying to bust his chops somehow. Oh, I wanted to quit my freshman year, of course. I wanted to leave. I wanted to get out of Alabama. I wanted to go anywhere."

After Alabama played Tennessee when Namath was a freshman, he sought out fellow Pennsylvanian Mike Lucci in the Vols' locker room, saying, "I just wanted to say hello because I'm homesick. I'm down here in the middle of Alabama with all these good ol' boys, and I wanted to talk to somebody from Western Pennsylvania."

McCollough said, "He was literally dropped in here, almost like parachuted into a foreign land, so to speak. He was a Yankee and he was different from the rest of the good ol' boys."

Steve Higgins said Namath somehow acquired a sort of drawl to blend with his Western Pennsylvania dialect. "Down South was a big influence. He'll tell you during his first couple of years down there he was thinking of moving back, but he really loved it down there, and he definitely picked up a kind of Southern little twinge."

As a liberal "Yankee," though, Namath was stunned when he encountered the insidious, prevalent signs of racial prejudice. He was incredulous to learn there were separate water fountains for blacks and whites.

In 1962, as a sophomore, Namath ranked fifth in the NCAA for touchdown passes; the culmination to the 10–1 season came with a 17–0 whitewashing of Oklahoma in the Orange Bowl. Alabama finished fifth in the final Associated Press poll.

Late in his junior season, as mentioned, Namath got caught breaking team rules, having been seen drinking at a party. Bryant promptly suspended him for two games. There was no talking his way out of this jam, not with the forceful Bryant in control.

Dooley remembered facing Namath in a 1964 game: "When he was in his senior year, I started my career as a [head college] coach against Alabama in Tuscaloosa. On about the second play, we sacked Namath. He had one green spot [grass stain] on his shoulder pads and never had another spot the whole day. He went 16-of-19 and never threw the ball in the fourth quarter because Bryant wanted to run it, so they just ran the ball on us. But it was a real initiation for me as a coach."

Alabama, in the meantime, wound up playing against fifth-ranked Texas in the Orange Bowl. Despite losing to the Longhorns, 21–17, the Crimson Tide's 10–1 record earned them the national championship, and Namath was the player of the game.

Namath's senior season also featured another event that altered his football future. In the fourth game of the year, he seriously injured his right knee on a bootleg play. Team officials simply taped him up, and he continued the season; however, Namath saw the difference: "I wasn't the same player. I knew that. I knew I couldn't run."

Namath's collegiate record had been splendid, but he no longer was a threat to run the ball, not with bad knees and not while wearing a cumbersome brace.

Dooley, more familiar with Namath than the rest of The Six, understandably felt Namath may have enjoyed the best college career of them all. "He had a heckuva career at Alabama despite some of his little challenges that he had to [face such as] conformity, I guess you would have to say, under Bryant. He had to conform and then in the end he loved Bryant because he had to conform and because he helped him so much."

Byrant appreciated Namath's help, too, and called him "the greatest athlete I've ever coached."

Even in college, Namath enjoyed flashing his sense of humor. Once a writer teased Namath by asking him if his major at Alabama was basket weaving. Namath's retort was, "Naw, man, journalism—it was easier."

Later he would come up with lines such as:

- On his birth: "I arrived in Beaver Falls for the first time, May 31, 1943, . . . I wore my hair short then."
- About Unitas: "I used to think Johnny was the best quarterback of all time. I still rate him one of the top two."
- About his love life: "If a doctor told me I had to give up women, I'm sure I'd give up doctors."
- About a love scene he shared with costar Ann-Margret in the 1970 movie *C.C. & Company:* "I wasn't a great actor, but I did have some experience with love scenes, you see. It was awkward doing the scene because there were people around. . . . Yeah, it was awkward, but it wasn't *that* awkward."

Perhaps it's easy to joke when you're famous and wealthy. New York Jets owner Sonny Werblin came from a show-business background; in true Pavlovian style, he salivated over the prospect of signing Namath, even at an exorbitant price. Werblin said: "I don't know how to define star quality, but this guy has it. When he comes into a game, people move to the edge of their seats."

In retrospect, the 1965 signing of Namath was one of the biggest factors for the success of the 1960s' AFL and its eventually gaining parity and merging with the NFL.

In any case, Namath was drafted by both leagues separately—by the NFL's St. Louis Cardinals (No. 12 pick) and the AFL's New York Jets (No. 1 pick)—triggering a bidding war. St. Louis began the figurative auction a bit reluctantly at $200,000, but the Jets countered unblinkingly at $300,000. Eventually a deal with Werblin was worked out and included perks such as a house for Namath's mother; scouting jobs for his brothers; a sleek, green Lincoln Continental; and lots of loot. All that in an era when many stars only earned around $20,000 per season.

Interestingly, the deal Namath agreed to now seems laughable, but then it was positively astronomical—$426,000 for *three years* (some sources list a slightly different sum), an amount Werblin claimed to be the highest figure ever given to a professional athlete in any team sport. According to HBO Sports, Namath actually received a salary of $75,000 a season for three years and a signing bonus of $200,000 plus all the perks. Werblin simply said of the payout that he was "very happy to do it."

Finally, Namath belonged to New York—strong arm, quick release, oozing charisma, gimpy legs and all. When Namath moved to New York, Jenkins wrote, "He was youth, success, the clothes, the car, the penthouse, the big town, the girls, the autographs, and the games on Sunday." He added, "Whatever Joe meant to himself behind his wisecracks, his dark, rugged good looks, and his flashy tailoring, he was mostly one thing—a big celebrity in a celebrity-conscious town." And the owner of the Patriots, Billy Sullivan, called him, "the biggest thing in New York since Babe Ruth."

While Namath's childhood idol had been Unitas, in many ways Namath was the antithesis of the conservative-living Unitas. They represent an off-the-field study in contrast, ranging from their hair and lifestyles to the comments they made to the media.

Namath, for example, relished all the trappings that went with his stardom. "I liked the clothes. . . . I was styling. I was a part of the time, man." As reporter Sal Marchiano put it, Namath "was Mick Jagger in a football uniform. He wasn't Pat Boone, and that's what America wanted."

The singles scene was meant for this Jagger incarnation. When Namath first went to New York, he asked a friend how he could "connect" with the girls of the city. The succinct reply was, "Just throw a lot of touchdowns, you'll have no problem." His daily routine often was one of football, drinks, women, late nights; then, the next morning, it all began anew. "He was the king of New York," said his agent Jimmy Walsh.

Teammates knew there were rules for the rest of them and rules for Namath, but he seldom if ever let his ways interfere with his game. Jets running back Emerson Boozer said Namath "did not miss a practice, but he enjoyed the night life of New York City."

Namath's Upper East Side penthouse apartment on 72nd Street was as flamboyant as Namath himself, with snow leopard skin material on furniture and a bedroom ceiling covered with a mirror. Dan Jenkins described the lodging as having "an Italian marble bar, an elaborate stereo hookup, an oval bed that seemed to increase in size with each glance, a terrace, and more roommates than he could count."

Namath justified his swinging lifestyle saying, "I believe in letting a guy live the way he wants if he doesn't hurt anyone."

Some found Namath's way of living refreshing. Hockey's Ron Duguay commented that athletes who came after the Jets' star and who then lived by the carpe diem philosophy were figurative children of Namath. "He made it okay for pro athletes to look flashy and party and spend money on good times once in a while, instead of pretending to be very straight guys."

At the same time, Cleveland quarterback Frank Ryan, who had just taken his team to the NFL championship and who was much more conservative than Namath, declared, "If he's worth $400,000, I'm worth a million."

Namath proved to be worth a lot more than a million. When the NFL banned facial hair, a shrewd and opportunistic Namath commanded a $10,000 paycheck simply for shaving off his Fu Manchu mustache for a Schick electric shaver television commercial. He was so high profile, he naturally had many outside interests (including acting in movies) and did tons of endorsements, once making headlines when he did an amusing TV spot for Beauty Mist pantyhose, which proclaimed their product could "make any legs look like a million dollars."

Still, there was just one talent that triggered all of his immense earning power. Author Robert Smith wrote that Namath, "seemed able to throw passes in his sleep," reason enough to earn him the biggest bonus "since the ransom of Troy."

When asked if signing such a gaudy contract put pressure on him, Namath reflected and replied, "Pressure just makes you go a little more. I kinda like pressure a little bit."

He soon told the media of his strongest intention, saying his driving ambition was "to become known as a good quarterback, not a rich one."

However, when he first reported to the Jets, he heard that an NFL player said he believed Namath, with his huge contract, might not be willing to "pay the price." Namath countered: "Can you believe that? Why, you can't play for Bryant for four years and not know how to *pay the price* for what you get out of life."

Writer Bob Carroll stated what everyone knew, that despite the fact that the Jets had also signed 1964 Heisman winner John Huarte out of Notre Dame, "Namath was the new Jets quarterback from the moment he signed unless his knee fell completely off." Given his serious operation in January 1965, the first of a handful of such operations, the less desirable outcome wasn't out of the question. However, Huarte never threw a pass while wearing the green and white of the Jets, and he ended his six-year career with only one touchdown to his credit.

Carroll noted, "Namath, with his good looks, ready quips, and love of New York's nightlife, became an immediate media darling." He was "the fan's ideal athlete—the talented youngster who played hard on the field and just as hard off." Even detractors of his lifestyle were amused by the title he later chose for his autobiography, *I Can't Wait until Tomorrow ('Cause I Get Better Looking Every Day)*.

After his 1965 operation, his doctor said that while things had gone well, he predicted Namath would be able to play for just four years in the pros. Namath, happy to hear things went smoothly, said he was even happier to hear of the four-year prognosis. "I'll take *that*," he thought.

In truth, Namath wasn't a "darling" or an "ideal" to everyone. There were many, including veteran members of the media, who resented Namath's ways, his white shoes and "his blatant self-indulgence (a llama rug in his over decorated apartment was deep enough to conceal a nest of rattlers)."

Some veteran Jets, hardly enchanted with the upstart quarterback, made snide, sarcastic comments about Namath when he reported to training camp—things like, "Oh, boy, now our Savior is here." They saw him as a sort of teacher's pet to Werblin.

Former teammate, defensive end Gerry Philbin, remembered: "At first there was an undercurrent of resentment—nothing you could pinpoint, but it was there—about Joe's money and his publicity. That was at first. It disappeared when everybody found out what a great guy he is."

In a documentary produced by HBO, Namath spoke of a team meeting after a practice session, in which "some of the guys, the veterans said their piece. I had to say something. 'Like me or dislike me all you want off the field. Don't bring it on the field. And if you don't understand that and you want to fight, then you can go ahead and do your best—I will fight.' Nobody attacked me. I didn't get in any fights right then, so they knew I was there to play football."

By contrast, coaches such as Ken Meyer were impressed. He said Namath was "the only quarterback I've ever been around that you didn't have to look to see when the ball was released—you could *hear* it. Whoosh. You could hear the whoosh when the ball left his hand." Some said his throws were like darts.

Teammate John Schmitt said Jets receivers "had black and blue marks on their body from getting hit by these balls that he threw." And wide receiver Don Maynard confirmed there was no hyperbole involved. "Oh, yeah, basically on my arms and biceps. You catch the point of the ball— kinda like getting hit with a hammer. I didn't have to see him work out but one time to realize that this guy's unbelievable."

The origin of Namath's white shoes is an interesting tale. Jets head coach Weeb Ewbank was also the team general manager, one who was as money conscious as a coupon-clipping housewife on a tight budget. Namath related: "He just got flat tired of me putting so much tape around my darn shoes. . . . I walk into the locker room one day and sitting right there on the floor in my locker was a pair of white football shoes. I had never seen anything like them." Namath had developed the habit of using so much tape in college simply because he liked a snug fit.

Neither had his bug-eyed teammates seen anything like it. Schmitt teased him: "Low-cut, *white* shoes? I mean, nobody wore white shoes. Joe, come on! What are you, dancin'?'" Namath, predictably, took to them immediately. "I liked the look—I knew it was different. I mean, that was *me.*"

Opponents quickly came to recognize Namath as a legitimate star. Jim Houston, a four-time Pro Bowler for the Browns, said that while Namath wasn't "quite as good as the others [The Six], he was a good one. I was a captain of the defense and we always had to consider what his tendencies were, but he found a way to deliver."

However, the Jets weren't propelled to *immediate* success. Namath didn't record the team's first win until their sixth game, and he didn't even start the first two games of the season. Yet fans flocked to see the Jets in Shea Stadium, and they were a better draw, by far, than any other team while on the road.

Ewbank recalled that Namath and his star receivers George Sauer and Don Maynard "would stay after practice. We called it 'special work.' They'd stay 15 or 20 minutes extra just working on the plays they thought would be good that week until they had them so precise it was wonderful." Ewbank said Namath and Maynard would, like Unitas and Raymond Berry, "ad lib" pass patterns during games, changing them on the fly via hand signals.

Maynard once explained how he and Namath were so effective on quick out patterns. In practice, they held a contest in which Namath attempted to get the ball to the spot where Maynard eventually wound up, and do so before Maynard took his three steps and made his turn. "Believe me," said Maynard, alluding to Namath's quickness and strong arm, "I always wore my helmet 'cause I didn't want that ball to hit me in the head."

Ewbank made one significant change to Namath's passing style. At Alabama, Namath had taken a five-yard drop back and tried to get rid of the ball in a bit under 1.5 seconds. Ewbank instructed Namath to fade back eight yards and wait as long as 3.2 seconds before getting rid of the ball. He also knew Namath would have to learn how to read defenses well, how to call audibles, how to hit his target on the break, and how to lead an NFL team.

In 1967, Namath became the first professional football player to throw for 4,000+ yards, and he accomplished that in just his third year in the league (his second as a full-time starter) at the age of 24. He remains the only man ever to reach that plateau in a season with fewer than 16 games.

Some critics called Namath "pass happy," an AFL bombardier, and argued that he didn't learn to attack defenses with all of his weapons—that is, until the Jets' fourth contest in 1968. In that game, he mixed the running game (40 plays) and the passing games (34 plays), something he did to perfection in that season's Super Bowl. Further, no longer forcing passes when it was prudent to ditch the ball, the new Namath led the team to an 11–3 record, an improvement of five wins over their showing from two years earlier.

Before the beginning of the Jets' contest versus the Oakland Raiders in November 1968, which came to be known as the "Heidi game," Namath reflected on a game between the two teams from one year earlier. In that contest the 6'8", 275-pound defensive end Ben Davidson had broken Namath's cheekbone. A few days before the two teams again squared off, the Jets discovered that a photograph of Davidson's wicked hit of Namath was displayed on a wall in the Raiders' offices. One reporter approached Namath prior to kickoff and asked if he felt Oakland would again be zeroing in on him. Namath replied, "If they want to win, they'd better be."

In the game, Namath wound up putting 32 points on the board while clicking for 381 yards, but a Jets team record of allowing 145 yards on 13 penalties helped give the Raiders an 11-point victory. So did Oakland's ability to score two touchdowns in nine seconds with TV viewers forced to stare at the children's show *Heidi* instead of the exciting conclusion of a 43–32 barn burner. NBC executives had decided to cut away from the game, which had already run nearly three hours long. It proved to be a foolish decision. With a bit over one minute left to play, fans missed the conclusion to a game in which the lead had already changed hands eight times. An instant classic was being created, even as millions were deprived of seeing the game's amazing conclusion.

Undaunted by the loss in that wild contest and shaking off any negative thoughts about Davidson and the Raiders, Namath, with his eye-popping quick delivery, threw for three scores the next time the two squads met in a much bigger game, the 1968 AFL championship game.

A throng of 62,627 crammed their way into Shea Stadium, ready to celebrate a win just two days before they celebrated New Year's Eve. Winds of up to 35 miles an hour whipped through the stadium. Clearly, it was not a day conducive to passing.

Shortly after the Raiders scored in the second quarter to narrow their deficit to 10–7, Namath trotted off the field with a dislocated ring finger on his left hand. The trainer warned Namath that what he was about to do would cause him pain, but the quarterback dismissed him, "It already hurts." The finger, which was pointed at a crazy angle, was pulled back into place, and a grimacing Namath returned to the game.

With eight minutes to play, the Raiders had taken the lead, 23–20. It was then that Namath took over and ultimately hit Maynard, throwing the ball sidearm for the game-winning touchdown, doing so after first looking at *three* other receivers.

If there were any doubt about his determination, that game proved his mettle, winning despite, as he put it, getting his "bell rung in the first quarter; [and getting] a little dislocated finger in the second quarter." Namath kept rolling on, every snap of the frozen football resulting in withering pain. Looking back, Namath called the game "the most physical game, toughest game that I'd ever been in—that we won."

Playing through pain was not unusual at all for Namath, who once said, after being battered about by the Kansas City Chiefs' defense, "I feel like I was in a gang fight all by myself." Winning a title game while playing with pain was quite a different matter, and the victory served the same purpose as popping a placebo. For the time being, the pain seemed to vanish.

The win punched the Jets' ticket to Super Bowl III, though the NFL champion Baltimore Colts felt the Jets would be better served if they simply stayed home. Joe Unitas, a cousin of Johnny, recalled that when "Johnny was getting off the airplane, the reporters wanted to know, 'What do you think about Joe Namath?' He said, 'I never think about him.'"

Having never faced a team from the old NFL, Namath was berated by one coach who said, "Namath plays his first pro football game today." There was more to come as the buildup to the championship game was filled with histrionics and controversy.

In his book *The Dallas Cowboys,* Joe Nick Patoski painted the word picture of the brash Namath: "The long-haired, hedonistic antihero of pro football stood in front of a crowd of six hundred people, holding a glass of Johnnie Walker Red in his hand as he accepted the Miami Touchdown Club's NFL Player of the Year award and predicted, 'We're going to win on Sunday. I guarantee you.'" No equivocation there.

Later, Namath seemed to borrow and paraphrase a line from an old television Western, muttered by actor Walter Brennan after he was accused of being boastful about his skill with a pistol: "No brag. Just fact." Namath's version: "It's not bragging if you can do it."

Interestingly, Namath said that as a youngster he was never cocky because of his brothers. "They wouldn't let me get a big head. Confident, yes. I may have come off as cocky, but the reality of it was my home life, and where I came from, did not allow cockiness."

Distinctions aside, Namath made good on his football warranty. In doing so, as Hank Hersch put it, he "silenced the hordes of AFL detractors and turned himself into a legend."

He also silenced his coach. Ewbank was quite upset when he discovered Namath, who had been named team captain prior to the season, had guaranteed the Super Bowl win. Ewbank asked him why a 17-point underdog (and some sources listed 19.5- and 21-point spreads during the days leading up to the game), would want to rile up the alpha-dog Colts, even after he had warned his team not to say anything "to make them excited." Namath replied: "You're the guy who told us we could do it. You got us believing it. So the guy asked me, and I just told him the truth, the way I felt."

Namath's legacy might have been tarnished a bit if Unitas, rather than his backup, Earl Morrall, had led the Colts in the title contest. For instance, Morrall missed out on an easy score when he failed to see a wide-open receiver in the end zone, and most experts and Colts players feel Unitas could have defeated the Jets if he had more time on the field than he was given. However, Unitas had pretty much languished on the bench all season, hampered by a torn tendon in his right elbow; that's where he watched much of this Super Bowl.

And, despite the "I never think about him" quip, Unitas did talk and think about Namath. Sandy Unitas said, "He liked Joe Namath very much. John said Broadway Joe was in New York City, he was young and single at the time, and John said, 'I don't blame him [for his lifestyle]. I'd wear those pantyhose too if they paid me that kind of money.' John enjoyed him—they'd kid each other and carry on."

Chad Unitas said his father didn't resent or dislike Namath, but he was was among those who were convinced Johnny U. could have defeated Broadway Joe in the Super Bowl. Chad stated, "He often said that if he had gotten in the Super Bowl a lot earlier, or when Shula [originally] said he would have gotten in there, then it would have turned out a lot differently. Shula told him right at the beginning of halftime, 'Get ready, I'm going to put you into the game.' Shula came to him, I believe toward the end of the third quarter, finally."

Earlier, when the Colts got the ball in the third quarter, Shula apparently changed his mind about when to insert Unitas into the game. Shula told his star quarterback he was "going to give Earl another shot or two, or something like that," related Chad. "I think he went back in and it was three-and-out. They ended up not getting the ball back until later in the third quarter." Chad recalled his father saying that he "didn't have enough time to do what he needed to do." Joe Unitas elaborated:

Earl deserved to get the start because of how well he had played the whole season, but Shula told my dad at halftime, "I'm going to give Earl another shot here in the third quarter on the [first] drive. If nothing happens, then you're going to go in." [After the three plays and a punt] Shula said, "Oh, that wasn't enough chance." Then the Jets got the ball . . . [and] were able to burn a lot more time off the clock. . . .

The story is Ernie Accorsi, who was a PR guy with the Colts at the time, asked my dad after the game, when they were leaving the locker room, heading out to the bus, "Do you think if you had started the second half that the outcome would have been different?" And my dad just looked at him and said, "Ernie, I didn't need that much time." So he felt they definitely could have won if he'd have gotten another drive or two to get what he needed to get done.

A lot of what he did as a player and [his] play calling, he would see different things and kind of set the guys [on defense] up for something that he wanted to do down the road. He didn't have the kind of time that he needed to do that—it made it very difficult—you can't just walk in there and start throwing touchdown passes left and right.

The exact rundown is this: Unitas didn't take a snap until 3:58 was left in the third quarter, with Baltimore down, 13–0. The Jets tacked on another three points, and Unitas led an 80-yard drive for the Colts' only score with 3:23 left to play. It was too late to concern Namath and the Jets.

Earlier, however, there had been a play that could have left the Jets fearful of defeat. They led, 7–0, when, on the final play of the first half, the Colts ran a flea flicker, baffling the Jets' defense. A wide-open Jimmy Orr waved his arms frantically, signaling to Morrall that he was unguarded in the end zone. Morrall never saw him gesturing and threw an interception. The game was held in Miami, prompting Orr to later lament, "I was open from here to Tampa."

Colts running back Tom Matte said, "It was just before halftime, and in the back of the end zone was the Baltimore Colts Marching Band with their blue and white uniforms, and they blended right in with our uniforms, so Earl didn't even see Jimmy, which would have changed the whole complexion of that game."

Now, would Unitas have seen and hit Orr? "Oh, yeah. No question about it," said Matte. "It was bad. On top of it, Earl threw it to Jerry Hill, and the ball was picked off for an interception." Matte still remembers Unitas pacing the sidelines:

> He was up and down. Personally, I couldn't understand it either. I think Shula was a little worried, thinking about John's Achilles tendon. Can he get in there and do it? But he was cleared to go. I thought he should have come in a little earlier just to change the momentum around, but that was a decision by the coach. I would imagine that a lot of people would be second-guessing Shula on that one, as I did.
>
> It was a tough day for us, and it's been a tough day ever since then because we were expected to win. You should've heard when we played all the other NFL teams, "You guys let us down. Let these guys beat you." We had to live with that, and it wasn't any fun.

Matte said that Unitas and Shula, a former teammate of Unitas during his rookie season, "sort of went at it" from the start, and Unitas told Shula, "You take care of the defense, I'll take care of the offense." Shula's keeping Unitas on the bench so long in the Super Bowl exacerbated things. Matte recalled instances when he would "run on the field to bring in a play that Shula wanted to run, and of course John would say, 'It ain't going to work—I'm not calling it.'"

Enough of what could have been. From the Jets' point of view, Super Bowl III was a game in which 25-year-old "Broadway" Joe orchestrated the tempo. He had overcome a poor start to the season—12 interceptions over the first five contests—to pilot the Jets to an 11–3 record. After deciding he had to change his pass-happy strategy somewhat, he took Player of the Year honors.

When Namath prepared to stroll midfield for the Super Bowl III coin flip, his emotions were charged. "I look across there and I see Johnny Unitas. And we start walking out there, and that walk—I had stuff going through my head, man . . . stuff going through my head since I was a little guy."

Unitas had, in fact, been Namath's hero, and one year in high school he wore No. 19 to emulate Unitas. "Joey U. That was me," said Namath. "Joey U., yes sir, when I started wearing No. 19 after Johnny Unitas, Baltimore Colts, great quarterback, and certainly I tried to think I was him when I was out there playing."

Dooley, however, noted a difference in the players' styles. "Namath had a looseness. You know, his body was sort of loose, as contrasted to Unitas who, everything he did, it looked like he was stiff doing it. It was just a difference in body movement and personality of the two—maybe that was reflected even in their body language." Unitas employed a sort of chop-chop motion as he dropped back in the pocket, unlike the more smooth stylings seen in a young Namath who, said Dooley, "had quick feet, but his whole body was loose."

At any rate, Namath was playing once again in the Orange Bowl, as he had done twice with Alabama, and this time he turned the place into an abattoir, carving up the Colts. He believed Baltimore, on a season-long roll, would do nothing different from what they had done all year, so he was well prepped for the meeting, knowing their tendencies.

He called few plays from the huddle, choosing instead to decide what to run based on the look the Colts gave him at the line of scrimmage, attacking away from the strengths of each defensive look. Namath took game MVP honors, even though his arm didn't get a big workout on the day. He was, though, prepared to pass with his oh-so-quick release when he sensed blitzes. He didn't throw for a single touchdown, going 17-for-28 for 206 hard-gained yards, but "he'd *controlled* the game from the opening kickoff." The Jets won so convincingly, there was no need for Namath to put up a single pass in the final quarter.

He beamed a Cool Hand Luke kind of smile as he trotted off the field, flashing a "we're No. 1" gesture skyward, a world-champion quarterback with a stunning 16–7 victory under his belt. Namath could now boast that he owned championships at the high school, college, and professional levels.

In 2013, he said he still feels the Super Bowl victory resonates: "A lot of us are underdogs in our lives; there are a whole lot of underdogs on a daily basis in all walks of life, not just in sports or in football. I think our victory was inspiring because of the way it showed an underdog can come through."

Author Brad Herzog ranks Namath the 40th most important sports figure ever, largely due to the impact of his win in the Super Bowl.

Some credit Namath's backup quarterback in 1968 for his development into becoming a thinking quarterback, not merely a thrower. That backup man, a mentor to Namath, was in his 17th season of pro ball. He was fellow Western Pennsylvania native Babe Parilli, and he had "not only seen it all, he knew how to attack it." In fact, in 1964 Parilli had tormented defenses, throwing 31 touchdown passes for the then-named Boston Patriots. That total stood as a franchise record until Tom Brady finally broke it some 43 years later. Experts felt Namath finally knew how to mix in effective running plays with precise passes.

Ewbank pointed out that, while Namath did receive an avalanche of publicity, "Joe didn't ask for that. He'd say, 'Hey, we've got other good players. Get them.' But all they wanted was Joe."

After the Super Bowl win, Namath returned to Beaver Falls for a dinner and a parade to honor him. All of the Jets flew in to take part in the festivities and to show their respect for their star. Namath rode in a convertible during the parade; at one point, he spotted a man known as "Sluggo," who was a popular figure around town. Ken Thomas said that when Namath spotted "Sluggo," who was "mentally challenged," he shouted for him to join him in the car for the duration of the parade. "This was a 'nobody' all his life, and Joe took the time to make him feel special. He did things like that without a lot of fanfare."

Thomas said there are sides to Namath that not enough people know about. "In 2008, our football coach Larry Bruno was in the start of dementia, so some of us got together, and we were going to have a reunion party for him. What started out as a little get together for the coach ended up with over 1,000 people from all over the country to honor him."

Namath couldn't attend because he had made a commitment to play in a golf outing for the University of Alabama that day. Thomas said Namath told the alumni association of the University of Alabama to donate $25,000 to the Bruno fund as a favor for his having helped the school out by playing in their golf outing. Thomas concluded, "He wanted to take care of the coach and Beaver Falls."

Thomas says Namath now comes in for a fund-raiser almost yearly. "He signs memorabilia, has pictures taken with people—so patient and so gracious."

And while Namath is far from being bashful, he is also capable of displaying modesty, shunning the spotlight. Thomas says that when Namath returns to Beaver Falls and takes part in the town's sports Hall of Fame, "Joe is so inconspicuous at these things. He doesn't like to be the main feature. He gets up and talks for a few minutes, but whoever is getting inducted, he wants them to be the star that night."

Higgins said Namath possesses "one of the most recognizable faces in the country, maybe the world. He's put Beaver Falls on the map." Despite all that, Higgins continued, "He is just nothing but nice and kind and humble. And when he comes into town, he doesn't like being in the spotlight. He likes sitting in the background, supporting other guys. He's comfortable in that position."

Coach Dooley also saw sides of Namath that are not often touched upon. He saw him as respectful and considerate. "I remember when he was doing some autographing [at an event] and somebody mentioned my name because I wanted to say hello to him, and as soon as he heard my name he just jumped up and hugged me. He didn't have any reason to—I mean I had no *close* relationship with him, but I think it was just kind of a mutual respect."

While opposing players tried to tee off on Namath when he first came into the league, showing him not even a modicum of respect, things changed as time passed. At first, players resented Namath's salary; hulking Ben Davidson said that back then quarterbacks were fair game, probably a lot more so if they were wealthy. He said Namath's quick release made it impossible for defenders to put on their brakes before slamming into him. "That's why we sometimes maybe accidentally hit him after the ball was gone. That's my story, and I'm sticking to it."

Of course Namath could be crafty, too. Davidson once hit him with a cheap shot. Namath calmly returned to the huddle and instructed his team not to block Davidson. The leviathan barreled his way toward

Namath, who then drilled the ball, hitting Davidson, whose arms were raised high, directly between his legs. Namath reportedly stared down at Davidson and said, "See you next play."

Later opposing defenses still tried to sack him, of course, but, Jets running back John Riggins said, "I'd never seen another quarterback when guys would come in, and they had a clean shot at him, and they probably could have crushed him, but they would *catch him* and almost, like, let him down—ease him down—to the ground. It was sportsmanship of a different kind. . . ."

Defensive end Fred Dryer, a teammate in Namath's only season with the Los Angles Rams said, "You want to put him on the ground, you want to get him out of the game—you don't want to hurt him, you don't want to jeopardize his career. . . . You don't want to hurt him, 'cause you hurt the game."

Even a defensive tackle with a savage reputation respected Namath. Thomas told the story—said to be hard to believe, but true—of a time the Pittsburgh Steelers were playing against Namath; one of the larger defensive players, a rookie, "had a shot at Namath for a sack. He was going after him hard to lay one on him as Namath was [starting to go down], and Mean Joe Greene picked this rookie up and said, 'Hey, rookie, you weren't going to hit Joe Willie going that hard, were you? I'm gonna tell you something, rookie, the reason you're making the money you are is because of Joe Willie Namath.'"

Clearly, opponents had grown to respect Namath—for good reason. For one thing, everyone knew the guy was tough, Western Pennsylvania–tough. Jets teammate Rich Caster once said that every week he'd watch Namath standing on the trainer's table getting both of his knees taped. "It was sort of sad to see because you really wanted to think that maybe one day they won't have to do that, but that wasn't the case."

Shortly after Namath played in his last game as a member of the Jets, before he joined the Rams, he spoke philosophically about why it seemed his 13-year stint there, and his best days as a quarterback, had gone by so swiftly. "Because," he said simply, maintaining his Hugh Hefner–like view of life, "it's been fun. It goes slow in a hospital or someplace like that. Outside of that, I've had so much fun that, hell, I just went from one year to the other having fun and they all flew right past me."

Knee problems forced him to retire at the age of 34 in 1977, a season in which movement and the accomplishments that had once been so smooth and had come so easily, as Dryer said, "laborious." Scars adorned his knees, evidence of five operations over his career, crisscrossing all over and resembling a road map. His mother spoke with a doctor who told her that, when her son reached the age of 40, "he will have the legs of a 70-year-old man."

Dryer reflected upon Namath's place in the game. "That guy was very, very important to the game of football as a cultural icon and how he brought professional football into the television era, and with it, a whole degree of excitement. There are great shooting stars, and the likes of him will never, ever pass this way again."

Few fans realize it because he was bigger than his statistics, but Namath played for only four winning teams in his career. It didn't matter; his name and legend were indelibly etched into NFL lore.

Even the usually staid Vince Lombardi had lavish praise for Namath. "His arm, his release of the ball are just perfect. Namath is as good a passer as I've ever seen. . . . he's a perfect passer." No hyperbole. Just fact.

JOE MONTANA

A.K.A. "The Comeback Kid"

5

SELECT LIFETIME FACTS, statistics, and records of note: Through 2016, Montana's 3,409 completions rank him No. 16 all-time; his total of 273 touchdowns is also the 16th highest ever; and his 40,551 yards passing stands as the 17th highest total in NFL history. His career quarterback rating of 92.3 is No. 13, and his 63.2 percent completion rate stands No. 15 even now. Only 2.6 percent of his passes were picked off (No. 22).

He led the NFL for percentage of completed passes five times, for touchdowns and quarterback rating twice, and yards gained per pass attempt once. Based on records going back to 1960, Montana is in the 13th slot for the most lifetime game-winning drives with 33.

Montana won almost 75 percent of his regular season games (117–47). In the more demanding postseason games, he still won 70 percent of the time, including wins in seven of his first eight postseason contests.

Montana was named to the Pro Bowl eight times over his 12 full seasons in a 15-season career. He was the NFL MVP, as voted by the Associated Press in 1989, and he was selected to the 1980s All Decade Team.

• • •

Almost since his days in the crib, when he was under the watchful eyes of parents Joe Sr. and Theresa, Joe Montana played one sport or another; he found he could always excel, even against older boys. Interestingly, he grew up on Park Avenue in Monongahela, the same street that was home to NFL kicker Fred Cox.

Joe's father was extremely attentive to him, supporting him fully. Stanley Fabin, one of Montana's closest childhood friends, said: "I think his dad deserves a lot more credit than he's got because, without him Joey would have never surfaced. He always put Joey in a position where he could succeed, excel. He made sure Joey had everything—when it came time to play baseball, he had the best glove you could get. On Christmas we'd get toys, and Joe would always get sports toys. One was an [electric] football field that vibrated, and you put your players on and they'd move." Another was Foto-Electric Football, in which two kids selected offensive and defensive plays, then watched the results.

Tim Stokes, a high school basketball teammate of Montana's, said Joe's parents "coddled him—and that's not a bad thing. He had special equipment. Everybody else was wearing hand-out equipment, and it really worked out for him."

Fabin recollected the emphasis on sports in the Montana household:

We were just like brothers. The first time I saw him was when I moved next door to him when we were both about four years old. My dad worked on the railroad and was gone a lot. Joey's dad took me under his wing because Joey was an only child. When we were about nine years old, he used to get us and a few other boys, and he'd enter us in basketball tournaments.

It was sports all the time. He lived to play ball. We'd get home from school and hurry up outside to play ball. We played tackle football with no pads on, and we'd do that all summer long, too. Joey's dad was the manager of the Civic Finance office in Monongahela, and his mother was the secretary there. They'd come home around 7:00. Joey would eat supper at our house, then when they got home Joey's dad would take us to something sports related. We never missed a Roundball Classic or a game at Monongahela High School when we were young.

David Sarkus, now a speaker and consultant, who was a West Virginia University teammate of quarterback Oliver Luck (father of quarterback Andrew), once served as a backup quarterback to Montana. He said Montana was one of the many youngsters who was cognizant of the Mon Valley's sports history. "Oh, he had to be. I think he was very aware of the Notre Dame history, too. He was aware of Terry Hanratty and the other quarterbacks in this area." It was only natural that a young boy growing up in the valley would hear of the exploits of the great quarterbacks.

Montana was the kind of kid who spent countless hours honing his skills—trying, for example, to be like a football idol of his, Joe Namath.

Many times he would go into neighbor Bonnie Kosh's backyard and, like Unitas before him, throw a football through an automobile tire that his father had suspended from a rope tied to a tree branch. Kosh remembered:

> Joey—we called him Joey—really didn't have much of a backyard. So he used ours, which was like a football field, and there used to be a very big tree there.
>
> And every night before we were allowed to play or do anything, we would go down there, I would swing that tire with his father, and Joey would have to throw the ball through it and not hit the sides of that tire. He was basically getting the technique of throwing that football straight through there while it was moving—that was a great target for him. And he practiced hours with that, hours. Daily and for hours. His dad was the force behind him.

Kosh's mother, Emma Polonoli, added: "That's where Joey got the accuracy, throwing the football through the tire."

That, and perhaps by throwing snowballs, too. Chuck Smith, a high school teammate who went on to set the West Virginia University record for the most assisted tackles in a season, said: "He'd see a car come down the road—he was up on the hill—and he would throw the snowball, and it would hit the side window of the car as it passed his house. He had that timing, that awareness, that perception." It was just like leading a receiver.

Kosh said of Joey: "You know what? He's just an awesome guy. He's got a wonderful personality; he was never a kid to get mad. And, as far as things outside of sports, there was nothing, because that's what they did. He was constantly with his father, and they just flowed from one sport to another."

Fabin remembered his midget league days with Montana. "Joey didn't want to play [at first], and neither did I, but his dad grabbed us by the back of the neck and dragged us up to the football field. It was sports, sports, sports, and schoolwork. Most of the time when you're around 10 or 11 years old, you're just trying to get the ball hiked without a penalty, but us, we used to pass the football all the time with Joey." Fabin was one of Montana's receivers and said that with Montana they outclassed virtually everyone. "We lost one game in three years, and that was 6–0 to Belle Vernon. A lot of guys around town thought he was like a sissy, a bit, because he'd get really upset if something wasn't going his way. I had to tell them, 'Hey, it's not that he gets upset because he's a sissy. He just can't stand to lose.'"

Smith added, "When Joe was in ninth grade, tenth grade, he was a frail young man, but he was just a natural athlete. Joe didn't like to get hit, of course, when he was younger—nobody *likes* to get hit."

Fabin continued his description of the young Montana: "Joe was a good person. He was very cocky when it came to playing ball, and some of the guys didn't like him because of that, but all the guys who play professional sports are all a little cocky. He knew he was good and he knew he could win."

Midget league coach Carl Crawley, who was also a college football official who worked two national title games, spoke of Montana's earliest days in organized football: "When I first got him, his dad was one of my assistant coaches, and we took him in one year earlier than we should have. He progressed just like any other kid that was young like that. Joe was a very quiet young man, but he was just like any other young kid running around."

Crawley said that Montana was a smart ballplayer, even as a preteen:

[He] always made such great choices. What I did when he was our quarterback, I put a pro offense in, and we had things set up where the quarterback had to make a lot of decisions. I had a lot of plays that were set up that could be a run or a pass, and he would roll out to his right or to his left; and if they stayed back, he knew to run the ball. Plus, he had a short receiver and a long receiver. And, being a right-hander, he could throw [while rolling out] to his left with accuracy, and that's hard for a right-hander to do.

I remember once he was in a pro game, and he was rolling out to his left. He got around the end, and I saw him make this little move like he was going to go out of bounds. The defender pulled up, and he shifted around him and gained another 15, 20 yards. He was a very heady ballplayer.

I guess by me talking to him a lot, getting him to think and to read what was happening at an early age, [it helped him] to pick this stuff up very quickly. If you've watched a lot of kids, you can pick up a lot of things that the super ballplayer just does that comes to him very easily. Other guys struggle to do things, and [the super ballplayers] just pick them up and act like, "This is everyday [stuff]. I can do this." And they usually do. Until he wakes up and really realizes that he is one of the elite, he thinks everybody has that quality, but they don't.

Crawley said that he recognized Montana's great potential by the time he was his regular quarterback, around the age of 11. "I can remember talking to his dad, and I used to tell him, 'You know, Joe is going to be an All-American.' He was picking [subtle] things up then. He was doing them very well then. He was throwing the ball to Mike Brantley, who went on to Indiana, and Paul Timko, a good receiver, and Donnie Miller. He put the ball right in their chest, and they were going to catch it or it was going to knock them down."

Crawley said Montana was different from "some kids who will reach a plateau at that age, and they will not progress any more, but he kept progressing all the way up."

That's not to say he didn't need some prodding occasionally. "There were times when he would be running sprints, and he would beat guys by four and five yards, and I'd climb all over him because I could look at his face and see that he was coasting. I told him, 'You don't do that. You run. You put out all the way to that line.' Sometimes he'd just look at me."

Crawley noted that Montana was both quick *and* fast, "There's a difference between being quick and fast, but he wasn't blazing fast."

Mentally, Joe was focused, largely because, said Crawley, "he liked to win. I was at his mom and dad's house at a party when Joe was with the 49ers. We were all at the table, having some drinks and food, and we were playing a kids' game that had shapes—the hearts, squares, stars, rectangles—and you had a timer on it, and if you didn't get the shapes into correct positions before the timer went off, they all popped out. I watched him; everybody else's pieces were popping out and they're laughing, but Joe's hand–eye coordination was so good. He put them in on the first go-around, and he stopped the timer long before the pieces popped out. He had quick wits. Very heady. Some people have *it,* and some people don't. He had it."

Sarkus and Montana were roommates at football camp prior to Montana's senior year, but his first memory of Montana involved baseball. "My dad took me to watch Joe pitch. Joe was probably 12 years old, and

I was 9 or 10, but I can remember Joe pitching at the old Mounds Field in Monongahela." Montana's scorching fastball helped him register three perfect games in Little League.

Some people joked that Joe got his prowess from having his mother split a banana down the middle for him, then slather on peanut butter to create his favorite juvenile delicacy.

People readily took to Montana, who was fun loving, but usually rather quiet; "a person that was to himself for the most part," according to one high school teammate.

Ulice Payne, a basketball teammate of Montana in high school, said, "He didn't date a lot in high school. He was [first] an athlete. He had fun; he used to water ski a lot on the Monongahela River. He was good—one ski and all that crazy stuff."

Payne stated, "Joe was an only child, but you wouldn't know it. In other words, he wasn't hung up on himself. He had an MG as a young guy. When he turned 16, his parents bought it for him. He didn't flaunt it. He wasn't big-headed. I'm driving my Ford Torino with holes in the floorboard, and he's got the two-seater, a convertible, but you would never know it." An MG versus a Flintstone-styled car—quite the contrast.

Montana's Finley Middle School basketball coach, Tom Caudill, said Montana was "a real likable kid. A very modest, soft-spoken kid—that was Joe." Smith feels Montana has stayed "the same guy as he was when he was 14."

Caudill continued, "I thought the world of him. In fact, I can remember in junior high when I had him in phys ed. We had special-needs kids involved in our program, and we'd be out playing softball. When some of these kids came up to bat, Joe was the kind of a kid who would help them and, in fact, if a kid was able to hit the ball, he'd make sure he didn't catch it. He'd tell teammates to let the ball fall in for a hit. He was very supportive of those kinds of unfortunate kids. I admire him for that."

Sarkus stated: "I remember Joe as just a pretty happy-go-lucky [kid], who liked to laugh and have fun, but at that same time he was introverted, and I think that was probably a part of his personality that was mistaken for aloofness. But he was just quiet and reserved. I think he was really a loyal teammate in a lot of ways, but introverted. He was very cautious about who he let become close to him. He was very guarded in a lot of ways. He only had a few people who he let get really close to him in his little inner circle—at least that was my sense of it."

Jeff Petrucci, a teacher and a high school and college coach, was Montana's high school quarterback coach. "I started coaching at Ringgold [High School] when he was in eighth grade. Joe was an unassuming kind of kid. He possessed great ability, but he was basically, I would say, sort of a backwards, little bit of a shy kind of a person. I don't know that he knew at his young age how good he really was. I mean, I don't know that *anyone* knew. No one knew at that point in time that he was going to end up being pretty much the standard that all quarterbacks are measured by."

Montana had yet to develop into a take-charge quarterback. Petrucci felt he led by his feats more than his words. "Without question. I mean, Joe's ability was above and beyond others. He's not a talker. He's not a rah-rah kind of person. He's a matter of fact kind of person."

He didn't need to be a hollering guy, said Caudill, "because of his super athletic prowess. The kids respected him—he had that leadership quality." Call it a quiet confidence. In a way, he was not unlike a Hollywood actor who says he is normally a shy person, but, when given a role to play, becomes a totally different person.

Big things were in store for him in several sports when he entered Ringgold High School, where he starred in basketball. Stokes said, "If you were playing basketball in the playground, and Joe was on the side, he'd be the first one you'd pick."

Fabin pointed out that "Ringgold never had a good team until he got there—he took them to the playoffs. Joey was always a winner." Fabin even felt Montana could have played professional baseball as a shortstop or pitcher, and says Montana reached around 90 mph with his fastball in high school. "He wasn't the fastest pitcher, but he changed speeds on his pitches, he had a good curveball, and he could hit also."

Fabin continued: "a writer for the Pittsburgh *Post-Gazette* wrote that Joey was the best all-round high school basketball player at the Western Pennsylvania playoffs. North Carolina State offered him a four-year scholarship to play basketball. Notre Dame offered him a scholarship to play football. Joey wanted to play basketball *and* football there. They didn't allow him to do that, so his dad told him to focus on football." Even though the Irish basketball coach Digger Phelps told Montana he would see what he could do to allow Montana to play both sports, his days on the court would soon end.

Payne said, "He was not afraid to take a chance. I saw this when we played basketball. He would try a pass that had a low probability of success, but he would still try it. His father would bitch at him for that, but he wasn't afraid to fail—he'd try it again. He seemed to be comfortable with who he was."

Mark Gorscak, a lineman at Ringgold for Montana, believed Montana was "a better basketball player during that time period [high school] than anything else." Notre Dame football teammate Ken MacAfee said, "He could stand underneath the basketball hoop, and from a standing position jump up and stuff it behind his head. I said, 'I'm not sure I saw that,' so he did it again. I couldn't believe it."

Fabin said basketball was "the biggest thing to Joey—we'd play basketball every night at the St. Anthony playground. We'd play till their lights turned off, nine, ten o'clock, and then we'd go to bed."

"Back then," said Caudill, "you played ninth graders for the most part in junior high basketball, but Joe was good enough I started him as a seventh grader. Joe's father would come down to practices and observe, and I believe he had an *awful* lot to do with his success."

In Montana's junior year, Ringgold won the Western Pennsylvania Interscholastic Athletic League (WPIAL) hoop title by knocking off a General Braddock squad for the second time they met that season. Ringgold drew them once more in the semifinals of the state playoffs. This time Montana fouled out, and they lost.

Fran LaMendola, Ringgold's basketball coach, said the following season he needed to punch up the Rams' offense, depleted by the loss of talented seniors from the 1972–73 season. "At practice one time, I said to him, 'Joe. Look, you got to shoot a little more.' He said, 'Coach, just wait—let everybody else get the plays.' This is just the type of guy he was." Unselfish, he was willing to take a back seat and allow teammates to enjoy some glory.

More important, said LaMendola, Montana felt "the team was first. He was more worried about the team than about individual accomplishments. That's one thing I always remember about him."

As great a quarterback as he was, things were not always smooth. Caudill said that when Montana's football training began for his junior year at Ringgold, "Joe's father had a little problem with [head coach] Chuck Abramski." Upset with the coach for not starting his son, Joe Sr.—described by Caudill as being "a man of very few words"—couldn't believe his son was sitting on the bench. Abramski, however, was livid about Montana's refusal to participate in his off-season weight program,

Pitt's Dan Marino dropping back to pass. As a junior, he averaged just over three touchdown throws per game. (Courtesy of the Univ. of Pittsburgh)

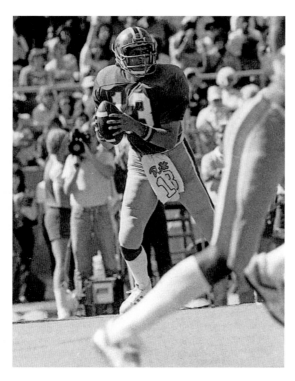

Marino shattered
virtually every Pitt
passing mark.
(Courtesy of the Univ.
of Pittsburgh)

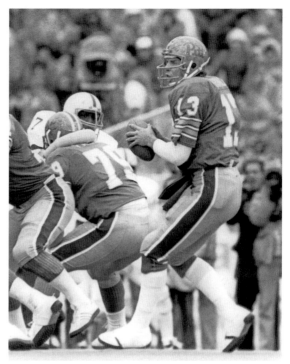

Marino's record at Pitt
was a stellar 42–6.
(Courtesy of the Univ.
of Pittsburgh)

Top: Marino celebrating Pitt's Sugar Bowl win in 1982 with receiver John Brown. (Courtesy of the Univ. of Pittsburgh)

Even as a freshman at Pitt, Marino starred (QB rating of 128.9). (Courtesy of the Univ. of Pittsburgh)

Marino with his head coach at Pitt,
Jackie Sherrill: "We didn't come
here to tie." (Courtesy of the Univ. of
Pittsburgh)

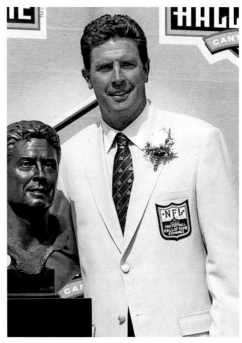

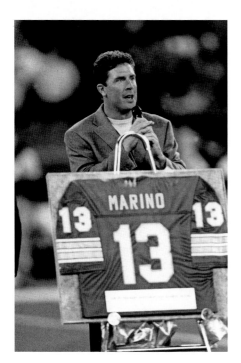

Top left: Marino at Pitt's commencement ceremony. (Courtesy of the Univ. of Pittsburgh)

Top right: Marino with his bust at the Pro Football Hall of Fame. (Courtesy of the Univ. of Pittsburgh)

Marino honored by having his uniform retired at Pitt. (Courtesy of the Univ. of Pittsburgh)

Montana in youth-league football. Even then, said his coach, "He always made such great choices." (Courtesy of Steve Russell)

Top right: Montana at Ringgold High School, with teacher Steve Russell and friend. (Courtesy of Steve Russell)

Bottom right: Joe Montana with Ringgold High School teacher Steve Russell, senior year, 1974. (Courtesy of Steve Russell)

Montana at a 2005 banquet.
(Courtesy of Steve Russell)

Author Wayne Stewart with
Montana. (Courtesy of Nancy
Stewart)

Top left: Long before Marino, Bimbo Cecconi held Pitt's all-time passing record. (Courtesy of Steve Russell)

Top right: Namath at Beaver Falls High School, encouraged by his head coach. (Courtesy of the Larry Bruno Foundation)

Namath back home at a Beaver Falls celebration. (Courtesy of the Larry Bruno Foundation)

Namath on the high school baseball team, first row, fourth from left. (Courtesy of the Larry Bruno Foundation)

Joe Namath was a standout quarterback with nimble, elusive running skills in high school. (Courtesy of the Larry Bruno Foundation)

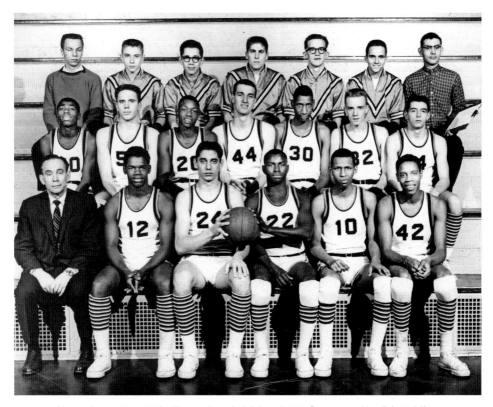

Namath as a basketball standout in high school, first row—No. 24, holding basketball. (Courtesy of the Larry Bruno Foundation)

Namath at a 1994 banquet in Beaver Falls—he always has maintained ties with his hometown. (Courtesy of the Larry Bruno Foundation)

Opposite: Namath on his high school football team, wearing No. 19, first row. Namath set numerous passing marks. (Courtesy of the Larry Bruno Foundation)

Sam Havrilak, like his Baltimore Colts teammate Johnny Unitas, was another product of Western Pennsylvania. (Courtesy of Steve Russell)

Fred Cox, the Minnesota Vikings kicker who grew up on the same street as Montana in Monongahela, Pennsylvania. (Courtesy of Steve Russell)

New England Patriots quarterback Scott Zolak—as a kid he was water boy for Montana's Ringgold High School team. (Courtesy of Steve Russell)

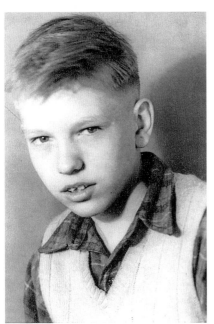

Johnny Unitas with his family. Some still say he's the greatest quarterback ever. (Courtesy of Paige Unitas)

Unitas as a middle school student. (Courtesy of Paige Unitas)

Unitas with his wife Sandy. (Courtesy of Paige Unitas)

Unitas with his daughter Paige and wife Sandy. (Courtesy of Paige Unitas)

Top: Unitas with Sandy and his sons Joe and Chad: "He's more proud of having his family than what he did." (Courtesy of Paige Unitas)

Unitas with his trophies, which didn't impress him: "I don't need all this stuff. I have the memories." (Courtesy of Paige Unitas)

choosing instead to play baseball and basketball that summer. So Paul Timko, a year ahead of Montana, remained Abramski's starter.

Petrucci commented: "The reason Joe was not playing in the first place was because Abramski could not deal with the fact Joe was not at the all-important weight program. Chuck's philosophy was if you did not do what he said year round, you would not get better. That was his biggest problem because other kids would see Joe not there and still play, so they figured they could miss also. He had to have total control, and Joe did not conform—not because he was contrary, but because he loved playing basketball and baseball."

Ringgold was blown out in the 1972 opening game, 34–6, won two games by way of forfeit, but lost a game they picked up as a replacement contest for one of the forfeits. Fabin recalled, "Joey finally got his opportunity, and he cashed in on it. All of a sudden, Abramski saw how Joey could throw the football and they passed quite a bit."

Actually, it wasn't quite all of a sudden. Yes, Montana finally got the starting nod, and footballs soon began raining down on Mon Valley football fields, but it took two events before that happened. First, during the preseason tight end Dave Osleger broke his collarbone, precipitating, perhaps to some degree, the *eventual* switching of Timko to that position. More important—and some say that this is actually the only event that led to Montana's winning the starting job—during a staff meeting Abramski's coaching staff finally convinced him they needed Montana to start. Abramski relented, and Montana started a scrimmage versus West Mifflin. He would never lose his starting job.

Petrucci commented, "We were not good enough as a team with Timko at quarterback and Joe on the bench." The collarbone issue, he insisted, "was not the reason the switch was made."

Contrary to Petrucci's view, Chuck Smith opined: "If Dave Osleger doesn't break his collarbone I don't think Joe would ever be a quarterback at Notre Dame or with the 49ers. Instead, I think Joe's dad would have taken him out to play basketball somewhere because of their conflict [with Abramski]. You talk about fate or destiny."

In any case, finally convinced Montana should run the team, Abramski watched on September 29, 1972, as Montana made his regular season varsity debut and went 13-for-22 for 255 yards. The Rams tied a much better Monessen team, which went on to register a record of 8–0–1, stunning them by scoring 34 points in the process. Three of Montana's four touchdowns that night went to Timko. Abramski beamed, "We could have passed on every down and gained."

Smith recalled, "We went into Monessen, the No. 1 team, and we jumped up on them, like 34–24 or something, but they came back and tied us. It was kind of a shocker because we weren't supposed to have all that great of a team. Of course, we just got better from that point on, and it was because of that one move."

The way Montana had first been used (or ignored) at Ringgold began a pattern that would continue at times throughout his career, especially with Coach Dan Devine at Notre Dame. Too often, it seems, Montana had to sit before he had the opportunity to prove himself. He met those challenges by not only displaying his talent, but doing it so well it vividly showed how ludicrous some of his coaches' decisions had been.

Actually, says Smith, the first pivotal moment for Montana to prove himself came when he had to, of all things, assert himself in a practice session. Smith related the tale:

Paul Timko played defensive end, and I was the other defensive end. It was the week Paul was moved to tight end, and he was upset because he was moved from quarterback. We had full scrimmage on Tuesdays, and Paul said, "I'll hit him [Montana] hard, Chuck. You hit him high, I'll hit him low."

I go in and grab Joe high, spin him around, and I just stopped him. I didn't hit him, I just wrapped my arms around him. I just held him there for a second. I knew we needed a quarterback, but the next thing I know, BAM, Paul came in and hit him. He hit him so hard that, due to the laws of physics, I took the blow! It passed right through Joe and into me because I was holding him. Then I'm lying on the ground, sucking for air. That's how I know how hard Paul hit him.

After about three times of that, Joe got up and got into a fight with Paul—threw the ball at him, and they started swinging at each other. From that point on, I think Joe took control and got a toughness in him that I never saw in him before. After that Joe just wouldn't take any more [stuff] from anybody.

Joe finally had enough, and I don't blame him. He got [ticked] off—it was one of the first times I saw him get so mad. It was a crossroads for him. From that point on, Joe had no problem leading that team. He'd get in the huddle, and he just took control.

You knew he could throw the ball, and, up to that point, we always said, "Don't let Joe get hit, or he won't be able to throw the ball." After that, Joe didn't get hit in a game or sacked very many times. And he could throw the ball back then in places that I just couldn't believe.

Once his teammates came under Montana's spell, they soon came to realize what Caudill knew so well. "You could always count on him in the clutch. That was typical of Joe. He was always a come-from-behind kid. That's the way he was when he played junior high basketball for me. He had the intensity and the love for the game. You could just read it on him—he was there to win."

Smith added, "Joe was very confident. He loved a challenge. When he came into a game, we knew that we were in good hands."

Ringgold could muster only a 4–4–2 record with several of those wins being via forfeit. As a starter Montana was quite talented—over his first three starts he threw nine TDs—but he produced two wins, two defeats, and he played to a tie twice.

Paul Zolak stated: "He always had the ability to get other people to achieve more than they thought they could achieve in the huddle. He always brought everybody up a notch because they had that much confidence in him." Zolak stated that a team cannot succeed "if you don't believe in the quarterback when you look in his eyes in the huddle." His Ringgold buddies believed.

Later, a 49ers teammate, Randy Cross, expressed a similar take on Montana. "There have been, and will be, much better arms and legs and much better bodies on quarterbacks in the NFL, but if you have to win a game or score a touchdown or win a championship, the only guy to get is Joe Montana." He was as steady, and as commanding, as a drill sergeant's cadence.

Smith said that, in one scrimmage, "we must have scored every time we touched the ball with Joe throwing and running. It was just unbelievable. Joe just lit up the skies with his passes."

During the regular season when Montana was a senior he produced an 8–1 record that propelled Ringgold into the playoffs where their most heartbreaking loss, 20–0 to Mount Lebanon, caused his high school career to screech to halt.

The game was played on a bitterly cold night, a precursor to the Chicken Soup game Montana later played. Fabin said: "There was a frozen drizzle that night so Ringgold couldn't throw the ball. Mount Lebanon kept their backs close to the line of scrimmage and just kept running the ball. They were very successful at running the ball, getting four, five yards on every carry. If that would have been on a nice night, they probably would have beaten Mount Lebanon."

Rich Lackner, longtime head football coach of Carnegie Mellon University, played for Mount Lebanon in that game, which saw temperatures around 0° F with windchill readings shivering at about 10° below. "A lot of their starting linemen [three starters in all] were out with the flu. Our head coach Art Walker and our defensive coordinator Mr. Ashburn found that out, and we blitzed the heck out of Joe. We took advantage of that opportunity. We knew he was a very talented football player, and he showed that in his throws that night. As the inside linebacker in the 4–4 defense, we were barreling all night."

Caudill said that when Montana suffered a loss, his reaction was subdued. "He wasn't the kind of a guy who would pound his fist on the wall. He'd get remorseful, but he took it like a true athlete. He took it to heart; it hurt him."

When Sarkus played for Abramski, the two of them once went to the Pittsburgh Steelers' training camp. "He took me for various reasons—one was to motivate me. I remember various passing drills. Terry Hanratty would drop back and pass, then Terry Bradshaw, then Joe Gilliam. Joe was either a senior or just out of school, and I remember Chuck saying, 'Joe throws as well as any of those guys right now.' Joe's arm was a bit underrated. He had a strong arm and quick release. Maybe he didn't have the bazooka that some guys had in the NFL then, but Joe had an excellent arm."

Even in high school, he possessed other great qualities, including "an uncanny ability to see the entire field." Sarkus remembered: "He could scan the field. The field slowed down considerably for him right away. I would imagine Joe was seeing things in slow motion. By the time he got to his senior year, he was always able to pick out a second or third receiver, and this is back in high school. I think that was one of his greatest abilities. He had great vision, great field vision. He had that calm about him that everybody later saw at the pro level."

Montana himself once made a similar comment. "What I have," he noted, "is recognition. The ability to see everything on the field. Position the other team to death. Keep the ball alive and keep it moving forward.

Then, at the right moment, knock them on their ass."

Sarkus continued:

He was mentally tough. Nothing rattled Joe. People saw Joe as this thin, skinny little quarterback, but Joe was physically and mentally tough. He got knocked down and came back. That was not recognized very clearly early on. Certainly, he had to be tough at Notre Dame and with the 49ers and Kansas City, but I think by the time Joe hit his senior year he was getting very tough.

Another thing people didn't see about Joe was he had great physical stamina. He could go up and down that basketball court all day. He could drop back or roll out six, seven times in a row and not miss a beat. I think his stamina was something that separated him from a lot of other athletes. Great, great stamina.

Petrucci saw Montana as a kid who "was very respectful of authority, and he was a very humble young man. He had great humility and ability. He was obviously blessed with those great abilities; he was good at anything, I don't care what sport it was; if he played it, he was going to be successful at it because he had that kind of ability." To Petrucci, this ability was not merely physical: "He was a highly disciplined player. I think it came from his parents. His whole personality reflected Joe and Theresa. He was their only child, and they raised him, teaching him to be respectful and be humble. He became that kind of an individual. He had that innate ability to be as good as he could be, and he was never going to settle for second place. He took great pride in winning and in being a team player."

Speer Ruey—who played high school football with Bernie Galiffa, a Pennsylvania All-State quarterback, and Ken Griffey Sr. at Donora High School—was also an acquaintance of Montana's. Ruey recalled a story that illustrates Montana's competitive spirit:

When they dedicated the Ringgold High School stadium [in September 2006], naming it for Joe Montana, Bernie came for the ceremonies. I'll tell you something I told to Joe Montana that really ticked him off. I just wanted to get a little dig in on him. I thought he'd take it OK. When he walked up to Bernie and me, I said, "Hey, Joe, I want to introduce you to the best high school quarterback I ever saw play." He gave me this look. But it was true—I think that actually Bernie was a better quarterback in high school than Joe was. Joe just got better once he got into college. As a senior I think Bernie was the best quarterback in the state.

The look Montana shot at Ruey may not exactly have been withering, but it was an extremely cool one.

The story displays Montana's burning pride that had served him well as a player, and it portrays his conviction that, even now, he—not Galiffa or *anybody* else—reigns as the greatest high school quarterback from his part of the state.

Petrucci said, "He's a coach's dream when it came to things like that. Very competitive, without question. Everything was fun to him—it was a game—that's what separated him from other players, even at the college and professional levels. He just had fun in the game."

Because of that attitude, said Petrucci, Montana didn't have to grapple with the concept of pressure; instead, he ignored it: "He didn't know what third-and-13 meant, that he had to make a first down. He just knew that the play was being called and that it was his job to get the ball to the receiver, and he was going to make that kind of play. He was that kind of individual. That set him apart. Plus he was very, very intelligent. He understood the 'whys' and what you were trying to do and the whole nine yards. He was a very good student in high school, and you can't be brain dead and [and graduate from Notre Dame]. He was very bright."

Even back in high school, Montana, in typical blue-collar style, simply did what he had to do, and he did it well. Petrucci put it this way:

He had a job to do, and he did his job, and he took pride in doing it. Everybody always knew, and the kids always felt, "As long as Joe's got the ball, we've got a chance to be successful."

Joe was born to be a quarterback. You saw it in the midget league, in high school, the electricity in the huddle when he was in there.

I coached for over 30 years, and I've never been around a player with such talent. He was also the best kid I've ever been around. You couldn't ask for a better human being than Joe Montana.

He was a serious kind of guy. He wasn't a jokester or anything like that; he was always serious. I mean he had fun, he laughed, but he was serious.

Ulice Payne saw a different facet to Montana in his younger days. "He was also a practical joker. He'd be the kind of guy who, at halftime, would tie my shoestrings together. I'd go to the bathroom, come back, and he would maybe tie my warm-up pants to something. Whatever the environment, he was probably the loosest guy. He was the opposite of serious business. He performed, he was a serious competitor, but he was loose—he was the guy snapping the towel in the shower."

Payne played against Montana in summer baseball. "He'd put dirt in your baseball spikes and crazy stuff, but he always competed."

Even as a pro, Montana confessed he was a prankster on occasion. "Nothing nasty," he said, "but I liked to have fun." In training camp when he was a rookie, unbeknownst to veteran players, he took some of the bicycles that they used to get around their huge training site and hung them high in some trees. He also let the air out of their tires and sometimes locked several bikes together using a chain. Another time, as recounted in Kevin Cook's *The Last Headbangers,* when he was asked to speak to the team, "Montana sucked helium beforehand and sounded like a duck."

Kidding aside, one thing coaches and teammates all knew was obvious: The young Montana was helmet and shoulder pads better than all his peers. Petrucci, recalling a prestigious high school All-Star game, said, "Are you kidding? When he played in the Big 33 Football Classic. On the first play of the game he was a tailback, and he threw a pass." The head coach of Montana's All-Star squad was from Central Catholic High School, and he had his quarterback in as the starter. However, the coach decided to open the game with Montana taking a pitchout and running around the end before fooling the defense with his pass. The coach even employed Montana as the punter for the contest. "He was an exceptional athlete," concluded Petrucci.

He was, in fact, so exceptional that he ended his high school era as a *Parade* magazine All-American. From there it was on to Notre Dame.

In 1974, as a freshman in camp, Montana led a group of young non-starters, running a dummy offense against the first-team defense. Vagas Ferguson, who would become a Notre Dame All-American, remembered:

It's almost like the first scrimmage. We were kind of nervous, but Joe surprised me how he took command, even at that stage, against the No. 1 defense. He got us fired up and that was something you don't really see, and I thought that was something very special about Joe. He really made us believe in ourselves. He had us running all over. He'd say, "Come on, let's show them what we got." He had us fired up, boy.

We ended up getting the defense pretty upset with us because he had us running all over them, and that got the defense in trouble. We were supposed to give them a good look, but we weren't supposed to make them look bad.

That was my first experience with him. He was so smooth, and he gave everybody confidence with just his presence. We thought we were playing a real game.

Ken MacAfee, a two-time consensus All-American at Notre Dame, said, "He was probably someone who should have played sooner than he actually did. He had a lot of charisma, but we called him a silent leader. Everybody had confidence in him to do the job, and no one ever questioned his ability because he proved himself over and over again with the comeback victories that we had, particularly in his sophomore year. That was enough—we didn't need any rah-rah type of guy with pregame speeches and yelling and screaming. If you were behind, you knew he had the ability to come back and win no matter what the circumstances."

Even when Montana was low on the depth charts, his talent was evident, but, said MacAfee, "you kind of get lost as a freshman in the shuffle at Notre Dame, at least back then, because you were winning national championships every few years. The competition was great, so it's tough to break in. He wasn't really noticed significantly by the coaches."

Notre Dame quarterback Rick Slager may know the secret as to why it took so long for the coaching staff to realize what they had in Montana:

He was not what I would call the greatest practice player. I think that if he had practiced the way he played games, he would've probably started as a freshman. The way I looked at it, it was kind of like you knew the talent was there, but, boy, when he'd get on a field in front of 60, 80 thousand people, it just went to a whole 'nother level. It was his ability to not allow anything to affect him other than to win, and he had an incredible drive to win.

I don't know if practice in college [was indicative of his talent], particularly as a freshman—I mean I was there when he was young, I mean really young—but in those years, there were probably a lot of distractions, and practice was practice. But, like I said, when he would get in, and it would be a game-type situation, there was a whole 'nother gear he put in place, where all of a sudden you knew, "Boy, this guy has something." I think that was part of the issue.

In 1975, Ara Parseghian was replaced as Notre Dame head coach by Dan Devine. After initially being listed fifth on the depth chart that year, Montana backed up Slager. That soon changed after he rallied the Irish several times. His string of collegiate successes began in the third game of the 1975 season, when Slager was hurt in the opening quarter against Northwestern. Down 7–0, Montana got the nod from Devine and promptly put points on the board. Notre Dame went on to win handily, 31–7.

He started the subsequent game versus Michigan State, but lost, 10–3. Back on the bench against the University of North Carolina, Montana was called upon to bail out a struggling Slager, this time with the Irish trailing, 14–6, with just 5:11 to go. After tying the game, he hit Ted Burgmeier for an 80-yard score to clinch the game with a tad over one minute left to play. Overall, Montana coolly fired the football for 129 yards and helped his team storm back for a 21–14 victory, only to find himself a benchwarmer once again.

Payne commented: "People didn't like Devine at Notre Dame. Joe was the fan favorite. They could never understand why Devine wasn't starting the guy."

Slager readily admitted, "He saved my butt on several occasions. He came in when we got into holes, and you thought at first, 'How lucky.'" After a little time, everyone realized there was no luck involved. One early example came when "we played against North Carolina, and he threw an out pattern to Burgmeier. The cornerback slipped, and the next thing you know Burgmeier scored a touchdown, and we're back in the game. There were just things that happened that were just unusual."

Montana had won one of the school's greatest comebacks ever, and still he rambled on. After the UNC game came that gem against Air Force. In the fourth quarter the score stood 30–10, prompting MacAfee to note: "Before Montana came in, we were being humiliated." After the stunning win, "We knew then that he had something special."

All Montana did that afternoon was splash a gaudy 21 unanswered points on the scoreboard to edge the Falcons by one. Finally, *finally*, he earned the starting job. He lost against the University of Southern California, then destroyed Navy, 31–0, before a broken finger ended his sophomore campaign.

Writers believed that the Irish would have had a mediocre 5–5 slate without Montana, not their final 8–3 overall record. Devine, for more reasons than his handling of Montana, had alienated many of his players, and they refused to accept a bid to play in the Cotton Bowl that season.

The 1976 season was a bust for Montana who was out all season, redshirted with a shoulder separation.

The following season, said Vagas Ferguson, Montana's skills picked up to where they had left off. "It was meant to be," Ferguson said. However, Montana's return did not begin smoothly. MacAfee remembered:

We were picked to win the national championship by some groups, AP, UPI, whatever. Rusty Lisch was quarterback, and everybody was kind of wondering why Joe wasn't starting. So there was kind of some controversy among the players. We went in and beat Pitt, the reigning national champions, 19–9, not a great victory. The next week we go to Mississippi and end up losing to them; I think they won four games all year.

The third week we played at Purdue, and we were losing so they took Lisch out and put Gary Forystek in. The second play he was in, a guy blitzed and broke his neck. Well, they put Lisch back in, and we're looking at the bench like, "Where is Joe?" Finally, after a couple more incompletions, they put Joe in.

His first pass was to me on an out pattern, and he threw the biggest duck I've ever seen. The thing was wobbling. A linebacker stepped in front of me, and it hit him right in the stomach, and he had nothing but 60 yards of green grass between me and the end zone, and he dropped the ball.

I went back to the huddle and said, "That was a nice one, Joe. You want to get it together and maybe throw a dart once in a while?" The rest is history. We won the game, and he played for the rest of the year. We never lost again.

When Montana got into the Purdue game in the second half, Purdue was leading by 10 points, 24–14. Notre Dame's sports information director Roger Valdiserri stated, "When Joe went in, our players on the field started jumping up and down," fully confident that it was Purdue, and not Notre Dame, now in peril. Sure enough, three scoring drives and 17 consecutive points later, Montana (9-of-14) put a much-needed notch in the win column.

Witnessing his play, critics wondered how, just days earlier, a healthy Montana could have been third on the depth chart. Some have speculated that Devine favored Lisch because he had recruited him, while it had been Parseghian who had recruited Montana.

Notre Dame defensive back Luther Bradley said that the Irish, desperately needing to pull out that win against Purdue, Devine finally said words to the effect of: "Okay, you're my guy. But we don't have to hug and kiss. I'll just bear with you. Because you're taking us to the promised land." It had taken a long time before Devine rubbed the fog out of his eyes to see the proverbial light.

His next big challenge came against the USC Trojans. Over the previous 10 meetings between the two teams, Notre Dame held a dismal record of 1–7–2, and even after Montana beat USC in 1977, the Irish would drop five more consecutive games to them.

In a ploy designed to psyche up his team, Devine had his men suit up in their green and gold uniforms for the first time since 1963. Montana threw for two scores and ran for two more. Final score: Notre Dame 49–USC 19.

Three weeks later, Montana turned a near loss against Clemson into a win. One of his receivers, Kris Haines, commented, "He was always in control of everything. We were behind Clemson, and we came back a couple of times to beat them.

"I played with a lot of guys and a lot of them were really cool customers, and those are the ones you don't get nervous with. There's an old saying, 'Nervous hens produce nervous chicks.' Well, you can kind of tell when a quarterback is nervous in the huddle—Joe was never one of those guys."

The team's regular season record was 10–1; even though they were underdogs entering their Cotton Bowl battle versus No. 1 Texas (11–0), they felt they could win and that a victory could earn them the national title. When linebacker Bob Golic was asked by a reporter in Dallas if he thought the game would end in a rout, he came back with, "Yeah. A rout for Notre Dame." He proved to be prophetic, as the Irish won by 28 points, 38–10. The national championship, their record-setting seventh, was in the books.

The win was a shocker. Ferguson explained:

People didn't think Joe was very good. They didn't think we deserved to be there. The media was all about Texas that week; nobody wanted to talk to us. They were 12 and 0, No. 1, they had the Heisman Trophy winner [Earl Campbell], the Outland Trophy winner [Brad Shearer], the best placekicker in the country [Russell Erxleben], and the two fastest wide receivers in the country [Lam Jones and Alfred Jackson], so everything was about them. The game was as good as won by Texas; we were rated No. 5 and shouldn't even have been playing them—that's what everybody was saying, and if you just lined us up, player-for-player, they would have just dominated us.

We weren't intimidated. That was the first time we were underdogs, we felt. That's fine with us. Joe got us fired up, "Come on, guys. They don't think we can do this. Let's go." Texas had a good team, no doubt about it, but Joe came through.

On the day, Notre Dame called 32 pass plays (Montana went 10-for-25 with one TD), winning largely due to the ground game: 53 rushes for 243 yards

Incredibly, the 1978 season began with the Irish losing their first two games; their 0-and-2 record, with both defeats at home, was their first such start in four score and two years—82 seasons. There would be no repeat title for Montana, but, as his center Dave Huffman put it, "We just picked up our jocks and went back to work."

Montana, never a quitter, took the Irish to 9 wins over their final 10 games. They again earned a trip to the Cotton Bowl, versus the Houston Cougars, which gave Montana a final chance to pull off a jaw-dropping comeback. He didn't disappoint.

The contest, which came to be referred to as the Chicken Soup game, featured what Huffman called "the worst ice storm to hit Dallas in thirty years. It was brutal and biting, and the fans stayed home in droves." He continued, "It was just flat-out freezing in the first half, and Joe was this skinny college kid to begin with." The windchill factor read a brutal -10°F, with wicked gusts ranging from 18 to 30 miles per hour affecting game play immensely.

After Montana opened things up by putting 12 points on the board in the first quarter, the Cougars rallied and took a 20–12 lead at the half. Entering the locker room, Montana was in the early stages of hypothermia. When the third quarter opened, he remained inside, wrapped in blankets and spooning down chicken soup as if he owned stock in the Campbell Soup Company. Fourteen more unanswered points followed, as Houston upped their lead to a commanding 34–12 score in the third quarter.

Ferguson remembered, "We started the second half without Joe, and when he got there, you just knew he was still kind of shaky—he shouldn't be playing, but when you're in there you just go."

He was unable to return to the field until there was only 7:37 left to play in the third quarter, and the Irish still trailed by an ostensibly insurmountable 34–12 deficit. But with Montana now a somewhat warm-blooded body, and with that blood circulating through him like an ancient god's ichor, he began his greatest comeback to date.

Montana took his reputation to Mount Olympus proportions as Notre Dame scored 23 rapid-fire, unanswered points, all in the final quarter, to pull out a stunning 35–34 victory. The Comeback Kid, as he would come to be known, had rallied his team in sensational fashion, earning MVP honors and capping his brilliance on the final play of the game, a play that began with a scant two seconds left, when he hit Haines to at last put the Irish on top.

Ferguson explained the end of the game like this:

We had to score to win. The last two plays of the game, we had an incompletion, and everybody looked to the sidelines to see what they wanted to do. They just waved their hands, Devine, everybody, like, "Run whatever you think you need to run." They were taking their headphones off, like, "Do whatever you want." Joe was going to do that anyway. [Ferguson laughed.]

Haines told Joe after the next-to-last play, "Joe, I can beat the guy." Joe got down on the ground on one knee and drew a play. "We're going to run the same play, but Kris you're going to run to the cone and I'm going to hit you right there in the end zone." We ran the play just like he drew it up with that deviation, and he hit Kris where he said he was going to. I was just amazed.

"We always say we can beat our man," chuckled Haines. "It was a situation where they were giving me the out. We scored a lot of times with that play all year. We worked on it a lot after practice. I had slipped on the play before, and I would have been open had I not slipped. So I said, 'Well, let's do it again. I won't slip this time. I can beat him.'"

The pass tied the game at 34–all, but the point after did the trick. Haines concluded: "You can't go out of your career, either one of us with a greater moment—to win the game on your last college play in a major bowl game. You can't get any better than that." Notre Dame ended up ranked No. 7 in the country.

His Notre Dame career over, Montana's fans could reflect on his stats: 268 completions on 515 attempts; 4,121 yards through the air with 25 touchdowns; and, of course, the six fourth-quarter comebacks he led. He graduated with a degree in marketing, but his next career move was inevitable—the NFL awaited.

Fabin said that Montana's being drafted by the 49ers in the third round meant that "obviously a lot of teams made mistakes by not taking him, but when Bill Walsh saw Joey, it was like that was what he had been looking for all of his career to run that West Coast offense. A lot of teams do that now, but back then he started that—the short passing. Instead of running the ball for three or four yards, they'd pass for seven or eight yards on first down. They passed the ball and passed the ball, and once they got a lead, they'd run the clock."

It's still an enigma how 81 players, including three other quarterbacks, were drafted ahead of Montana that year. It's equally puzzling, according to Allan Maki, how he "was considered too slight and his arm strength rated only 'average' by NFL scouts." For his part, Walsh was so impressed with Montana that he drafted him ahead of Steve Dils, a player he had coached at Stanford in 1978 when Dils won the Sammy Baugh Trophy, given to the nation's top passer.

Walsh certainly knew Montana was ideal for his ball-control attack, utilizing short passes that hurt their opponents like the cumulative effect of multiple piranha bites. Kevin Cook wrote that Walsh knew that "Montana had the feet, the discerning eye, and more. He had presence."

Fred Cox said, and not by way of criticism: "Montana probably had the weakest arm of [The Six]. That's all relative. I'm not saying he had a bad arm; he just didn't have the same gun that the rest of them had, but he was a much quicker passer. He was an extremely accurate passer. So for what each one of them [The Six] didn't have, they had two other things that they were the best at."

San Francisco quarterback coach Sam Wyche liked Montana. "What really impressed us was that he could immediately put into practice any coaching suggestion. He would literally eat the words right out of your mouth. Call it what you will—intelligence, intangibles, charisma—that's what we saw in Joe."

The 49ers' 1978 record was 2–14, and they repeated that dismal record in Montana's rookie year, in which he played behind Steve DeBerg and started just one game. Then, in 1980, they improved to 6–10, with Montana getting seven starts and becoming the undisputed starter by season's end.

He even posted the first of his fourth-quarter NFL comeback victories, a December 7 win over the New Orleans Saints. In that contest, the 49ers trailed at the half, 35–7, but scored four unanswered touchdowns, then kicked a field goal to win, 38–35, in overtime.

After the stunner, Walsh remarked, "That was really Joe's breakout game. That gave him the confidence he could do the job."

"Joe Cool"—another of Montana's well-earned nicknames—arrived big time in 1981, his first full season as the starter, taking the team to a glittering 13–3 record, tops in the NFL. After he led the 49ers to a December win over Cincinnati, Bengals linebacker Reggie Williams remarked: "He would find a way to foil you. He'd dodge, or let you get *this close* and then flick the ball away. We thought he was lucky at first, but he kept doing it. Finally you say he's just special, a true nemesis, the guy who makes you lose." Other observers noted that, for Montana, "time seemed to slow down when it mattered most."

For the second straight year, he led the NFL in percentage of passes completed. He would achieve that honor three more times. In fact, during 4 of the 10 seasons in which he started 11 or more games, he was the league's most accurate passer.

During the first playoff game of the 1981 season, Montana compiled a record 111 yards passing on the team's *first drive* against the New York Giants. Two penalties on the 49ers made the more-than-100-yards feat possible.

Much more to the point, his 49ers went on to win it all that season. Of course, one moment from the season that stands out is "The Catch" by Dwight Clark. Staging yet another great comeback, Montana drove the 49ers down to the Dallas six-yard line in the NFC championship game. The play "Brown Left Slot–Sprint Right Option" was called. Montana stuck the dagger deep into the Cowboys with his pass thrown off his right foot, dramatically coming after he had rolled to his right, being pursued by two smoke-snorting Cowboys. Clark soared to make the catch, scoring the game winner with 0:47 showing on the clock, on a pass that Montana later described as one he *thought* had been a bit high because he didn't actually see the ball's flight—he had simply lobbed the ball, not to Clark per se, but to *where he thought Clark would be.*

He had completed six of eight passes on the 89-yard drive, which had begun with 4:54 left to play. "I was very confident in the huddle. We had to move the ball, and we knew we could," he later commented.

"The Catch" created instant history; Montana stated that from then on "things began to change because we had set a standard of our own play that we [maintained]."

One other thing: Montana succeeded even though he had been informed that someone had made a phone call earlier that day, saying he was headed to the game with the intention of shooting Montana. Although naturally disturbed by the death threat, at one point Montana turned to his teammates and "joked glumly that he didn't want to run any more naked bootlegs." His sense of gallow's humor continued when he asked, "Anybody want to trade jerseys?"

With the 28–27 victory, the 49ers were headed to the first Super Bowl in franchise history. As Montana left the field, Cowboy defensive end Ed "Too Tall" Jones approached him saying, "You just beat America's Team." Montana, the competitor, the victor, replied, "Well, you can sit at home with the rest of America and watch the Super Bowl on TV."

The 49ers' win in Super Bowl XVI in January 1982 began auspiciously with their taking a 20–0 lead over the Bengals at the half. Montana went 14-for-22, won the MVP, and his team held on for a 26–21 decision. That was the same season in which he had reeled off a then-record five consecutive games with 300+ yards.

Montana's second Super Bowl win in January 1985 was a 38–16 rout over Marino's Dolphins. Montana, who wound up with 331 yards passing, threw for three touchdowns and took one in himself from six yards out. Counting the postseason, the 49ers went 18–1 on the year. Only a 20–17 loss to the Steelers in mid-October prevented them from posting a flawless record.

Miami defensive coordinator Chuck Studley praised Montana, saying: "There's nobody else like him. The way he knows where he is, where his receivers are, that complete vision he has—it's unbelievable."

Montana faced a threat to his career early in the 1986 season when he had to have back surgery, but he bounced back just seven weeks later and helped the 49ers win yet another division title.

In 1987, the 49ers went 13–2, and Montana won his first passing title with a 102.1 rating. Over a two-game stretch, he fired 22 consecutive passes without missing his target, a record since broken. He topped the league in touchdown passes just as he had in 1982, but San Francisco didn't make any noise in the postseason.

No noise—but there were simmering repercussions to Walsh's yanking Montana from their opening round playoff loss to the Vikings in favor of Steve Young. When mid-November of the 1988 season rolled around, the 49ers barely had their heads above the level of mediocrity with a 6–5 record. Walsh once again considered using Young over Montana, hurting Montana's pride and rousing his competitive nature.

His response was typical Montana-esque: he hoisted the team onto his shoulder pads, executing his offense to perfection while carrying the 49ers to a win in Super Bowl XXIII over the Bengals. He capped it all off with a long, 11-play drive—"The Drive"—during which he connected on eight of nine passes as the clock whittled down toward 00:00.

A quick recap: San Francisco trailed when the final quarter began, 13–6, but a Montana–to–Jerry Rice strike tied things up. Later, down by a score of 16–13, their famous trek downfield began with 3:10 on the clock; Montana's game-winning 10-yard TD pass to John Taylor, on the receiver's only catch of the day, came with 34 seconds remaining on the clock. Taylor, his secondary target, was in the middle of the end zone on the "20 Halfback Curl X-Up" play Montana had called. Yet again, he had taken the 49ers from a deficit to a remarkable 20–16 victory. He would later call the clinching play his biggest Super Bowl thrill ever.

Two interesting anecdotes came out of the waning moments of the game. When the 49ers began their last possession so far away from a much-needed score, one Bengal turned to wide receiver Cris Collinsworth and beamed, "We got them now." Collinsworth shot a glance at him, then replied, "Have you taken a look at who's quarterbacking the San Francisco 49ers?" He later marveled: "Joe Montana is not human. I don't want to call him a god, but he's definitely somewhere in between. Every single time he's had the chips down and people are counting him out, he's come back."

During what one writer labeled an "82-yard double-time march on a steamy Miami night," San Francisco called their second timeout of the drive. Then Montana, in the huddle, suddenly and unexpectedly said to his weary teammates, "Hey, look over there. There's John Candy." Indeed, Candy was sitting in the stands.

Paul Zolak said, "They're getting ready for the biggest drive of his career, and he's cool enough to say that and loosen everybody up. He led by example—no high five, he just led by example." Typical Western Pennsylvania style: substance over flamboyance, with a dash of composure thrown in.

Due to a holding penalty, the drive actually covered more than 82 yards. Montana accounted for 97 yards on eight of nine passing, and only five yards of the drive came on runs. After the game, his center, Randy Cross, stated, "In the huddle guys were saying, 'I can do it,' and we were telling them, 'Not *can* do it. You're *gonna* do it.'"

Television color commentator Joe Starkey called Montana an "absolute surgeon on the football field," then, switching metaphors, said Montana's performance was "almost like poetry."

The win marked their third championship of the decade and the only time Montana played in a Super Bowl but wasn't named the MVP. His Super Bowl record of 357 yards and the fact that most people felt he was the key to the final, do-or-die drive weren't enough. Rice won the trophy, establishing Super Bowl records for receptions (11) and yards via catches (215).

The 1989 regular season, an MVP year for Montana, was probably his best showing ever. He went 271 of 386 passing for 3,521 yards and 26 TDs versus only 8 interceptions, giving him a quarterback rating of 112.4, a new record and easily the best rating of his career—some 10.3 points higher than in 1987, the other time he led the league in that category. It's still the ninth best rating for a single season. He also led the league in 1989 by completing 70.2 percent of his passes, which still places him seventh ever.

Kevin Cook wrote that San Francisco was so efficient "their record on the road during the '80s was better than any other team's *home* record."

After winning their fifth consecutive NFC West Division title, San Francisco crushed the Minnesota Vikings in their first playoff game, 41–13, behind a sizzling Montana (17-of-24 with four TDs). Next, they rolled over the Los Angeles Rams, 30–3, as Montana threw 30 passes and missed his target just 4 times.

Finally, Super Bowl XXIV belonged to San Francisco as they annihilated the Denver Broncos, 55–10, to lift their overall season record to a gaudy 17–2. Their point total set a new Super Bowl standard as Montana guided the well-oiled machine to touchdowns on four of the team's first-half drives. He completed 22 of his 29 throws, coming up just three yards shy of the 300 mark, and his 5 touchdown throws set a new Super Bowl record. As a matter of fact, his quarterback rating that day of 147.56 is still the second best ever. In postseason action that season, Montana put a whopping 126 points in the books, and the defense gave up just 26 points.

Montana was racking up postseason trophies and rings with a regularity that bordered on the ho-hum routine. The 49ers had captured their second straight Super Bowl and their fourth Lombardi Trophy over a nine-year span. Domination.

Montana finished his Super Bowl days having never thrown an interception in the big game, even though he put the ball in the air 122 times. At one point, Montana even held the following single-game and career Super Bowl records:

- most lifetime passes completed (83, still tied for No. 3)
- career completion rate (68 percent, just two percentage points behind Troy Aikman; still No. 3)
- most yards passing in a game (357, still tied at No. 5)
- career yards through the air (still No. 3—only Tom Brady and Kurt Warner own more Super Bowl passing yardage than Montana's 1,142)
- most touchdown passes in a game (5, still No. 2)
- career touchdown passes (11, trailing only Brady now)
- most consecutive completions in a game (13, versus Denver; still No. 2 behind Brady)

In Super Bowl XXIV, he clicked on 75.9 percent of his passes, topped then only by Phil Simms, and still the third best single game Super Bowl percentage.

You take a team to four Super Bowls while throwing 45 postseason touchdowns, which was once the highest total ever, and people take heed. Montana averaged almost exactly two touchdown passes for each playoff game he appeared in (23). His postseason quarterback rating stands at 95.6—by way of comparison, Brady's rating is 89.0.

Win all four of your Super Bowl appearances, while copping that game's MVP on three occasions, and you're an all-time elite. You still hold the record for the loftiest passer rating in Super Bowl play at 127.8. Toss in a few other remarkable feats like winning almost exactly 70 percent of all your playoff games, and many experts peg you as the greatest quarterback of all-time. Montana even registered passer ratings of 100+ in each of his Super Bowl contests. What else can you say, but to echo Rick Slager: Montana was at a "whole 'nother level."

In 1990, the 49ers started the season with a franchise record 10 wins in a row; in one game, Montana fired the football for a team record 476 yards. The team went 14–2 on the year, but Montana was injured in the NFC championship loss to the Giants. This began a skein of physical problems that signaled Montana's days with the 49ers were through. Eventually, the team went with quarterback Steve Young, five years younger than the 36-year-old Montana.

After two seasons playing for the Chiefs, both years resulting in trips to the playoffs, where Montana once again engineered several more dramatic comeback wins, he retired at the end of the 1994 season. Montana wound up with a total of five game-winning drives in playoff action, third best ever.

His playing days over, Montana owned countless team and league records, including playoff marks for completions, yards, and touchdowns, making him the ultimate money player.

Marino summed up what he admired most about Montana: "Every opportunity he's had to win, Joe's done what he had to do to win. . . . He's been in four Super Bowls, and he could have won two and lost two, but he's won all four. He was a big-time player, and he played great in big ballgames."

Many people have analyzed the ingredients of Montana's greatness. Scott Zolak came up with: "Smooth. He had evadability—I know it may be a made up word, but it's that knack to have a clock in the head. He was phenomenal—that one little step before the pass. He knew where the pressure was coming from, and he knew how to evade it. He knew how to buy time; and he was accurate. Evadability and accuracy—the two best traits you can have as a quarterback, and he had both of those."

Vince Dooley saw a comparison between Unitas and Montana: "He's another example of misjudging. Montana was a third-round draft choice, but he just had that innate ability to win when the game was on the line. He just made the plays—he could make plays when the game was on the line more so than any quarterback I can remember."

Dooley likened Montana to a torrid baseball hitter when the ball seems as big as a cantaloupe or a basketball player in the middle of a shoot-the-lights-out streak. Often, everything Montana threw was right on target, as if he were figuratively unconscious. "Yeah, when he gets into that groove, he was in the zone, so to speak. You could put it a lot of different ways, but he made plays when he had to."

In his estimation of Montana's greatness, Fred Cox simply said:

I don't know how you could do anything but put him right up there with all of the all-time greats. With as many championships as he won, as great a career as he had, as many touchdown passes as he had. People can blow that off and say he had great receivers and great everything else, but it doesn't matter how great you are; if you play for a bad team, you're never going to be great. To be great, you have to [excel and] play for a good team, or at least a decent team. Joe was fortunate, much like Fran Tarkenton, that he played for good football teams so he had the opportunity to throw a lot of touchdown passes, win a lot of games, and win championships. But in my opinion, San Francisco doesn't win those championships without Joe Montana.

When Montana was ushered into the Pro Football Hall of Fame in 2000, he commented: "I think the one thing that I continue throughout my life is that wish to be perfect. The need for perfection." He nearly achieved that goal on the gridiron.

Rick Slager described his view of how Montana, ever striving for perfection, always managed to maintain balance and poise:

We were competing against one another. Joe was an incredibly competitive person, and yet we had a very good relationship. We roomed together on a lot of the away trips. When people ask me about him, I've always said that there was something, a gift, that he was born with that most people are not, which was really a gift that allowed him to be incredibly competitive and at the same time almost unaffected by everything around him, which led to a calmness.

When he would walk into a huddle, it was very different than any kind of quarterback interactions with the team that I had ever seen, because it was an air of confidence, without it being prideful or boastful. It was a sense of "We're going to get this done so everybody just relax and calm down." I think it was his leadership gift. A lot of people are real fiery, a lot of people get down, get nervous, but he seemed to just rise to those occasions to a level that was uncanny. It was a gift that he had that was very special. And you knew that anytime that he was playing, there were going to be some really interesting things that were going to happen because he was unflappable. You just could not get him to think negatively. He brought that air of confidence, and it wasn't even spoken, it wasn't a spoken thing, it was demeanor.

Cox described Montana's poise and confidence in another way:

This is not a put down, because I tell people about Tarkenton being this way, too: everybody thinks that professional quarterbacks have a major ego problem. Well, the bottom line on it is: If you're going to be a great NFL quarterback, you better have a big ego. You better be able to throw three interceptions in a game and know that your next pass is going to be a touchdown.

Joe was like that, and Tarkenton, who I was very close to, was just the same, but that's the way it is. If you don't have that kind of attitude in pro ball, you just can't play and be worried about whether you're going to throw an interception. You're just not going to get it done. That's like a kicker worried about his last miss. If you worried about the last one you kicked—if you're even thinking about the last one, whether you made it or missed it, you're in trouble on your next kick.

Scott Zolak agreed. "But just don't let it get out of control. It's your team— you gotta believe it's your team. That's what comes with the ego, but I think some guys like Ryan Leaf, that's ego, but that's a different kind of ego. If you're able to harness it at a young age, you can be effective at what you do, you can go a long way."

Zolak said Montana possessed a "command of the room, he walks in—it's not cocky, it's a kind of swagger. [It's remarkable] when you can step in a huddle when things are frantic and situations are bad, maybe late in the game—like Joe did down in that Super Bowl in Miami when he said, 'Hey, look. There's John Candy.' In moments where most people panic, he thrives."

One aspect of Montana that may have been slightly overlooked was his passing style and touch. Ferguson said, "You knew if he threw it, you were going to catch it. The kind of balls he threw, you didn't worry about catching them—it was that special touch he had. I've been around a lot of quarterbacks, and I've never seen anybody throw the ball like he did. He's not one of those guys that burned you up with the football—make a catch and it'd knock you down."

MacAfee concurred. "He threw a great ball. You could tell it was kind of a softer pass—a lot of guys try to whip it in there as hard as they could, so hard you could hardly catch it." He continued his critique, praising "Joe's accuracy and his ability to deliver the ball with a spiral, and nice, soft passes whether they were 10- or 40-yard passes."

His greatness is a given, no surprise there, but a passel of observers of Montana are astounded at how down-to-earth he has remained, unlike so many superstars. Ferguson said, "If you saw him out of uniform, you probably would have thought he was a ball boy, the way he carried himself. He wasn't one of those kinds of guys you noticed." Nor did he demand to be noticed.

Before the Cotton Bowl game versus Texas, related MacAfee, "there was a lot of talking back and forth in the media. Joe never said anything. He just let his abilities do the talking on the field. I'm convinced we never would have won the national championship if it wasn't for Joe."

Humble, yes, but proud, too—after all, this was a man who performed his "Montana Magic" to perfection: he started 11 or more games 10 times in his career, and he took his teams to the playoffs 11 times overall.

As his midget league coach noted, the one thing people most associate with Montana is this: "If you watched him play, as long as there was time on the clock, he never gave up."

In 2006, *Sports Illustrated* selected him as the *greatest clutch quarterback of all time.* Not bad: it says a lot when a person's resume can be summed up in just six words.

San Francisco 49ers owner Eddie DeBartolo Jr. paid tribute to Montana by saying, "Excellence wasn't an accident for Joe. It was a habit, a singular act of talent and discipline." He continued: "Whether 15 minutes or 15 seconds remained, Joe always maintained the same level of composure. He was a leader, the hero you always wanted to emulate and a legend to behold."

DAN MARINO

"We Didn't Come Here to Tie"

SELECT LIFETIME FACTS, statistics, and records of note:
Upon Marino's retirement, he owned the NFL records for passing yardage, most completions and attempts, and most touchdowns. Nine times he was voted to the Pro Bowl over his 17 seasons, and on three occasions he was a first team All-Pro. As a matter of fact, coming off his 1983 Rookie of the Year season, he was the first rookie to ever start a Pro Bowl contest.

Marino (through 2016) stands No. 5 on the all-time list for the most lifetime completions with 4,967, and he also ranks fifth for touchdowns (with 420) and fourth for career passes attempted. He is also fifth best in an obscure, but admirable realm—the most fourth-quarter comebacks in a season (six in 1992). Only five men, including Western Pennsylvania's Joe Montana, produced more game-winning drives in postseason play than Marino's four such marches.

Marino averaged 34.5 passes (No. 11) and 253.6 yards through the air per game (No. 11). He's 20th on the list of passes completed per game at 20.5, and he completed 59.4 percent of all his passes.

He won the Offensive Player of the Year Award in 1994, one year after a torn Achilles halted his 145 consecutive games played streak. His quarterback rating of 86.4 stands No. 26 in NFL history.

The first man to throw for 5,000+ yards in a season, Marino left pro football as its all-time leader for yards passing with an incredible 61,361 yards, a total still lofty enough to rank No. 5 in NFL annals.

• • •

Dan Marino possessed a great arm, just like fellow Pittsburgher Unitas. Not only do they both hail from the same city, upon their retirement each one ranked first on several all-time lists, including most touchdowns thrown, most completions, and most yards through the air. They also share the middle name "Constantine." According to those who have known him the longest, Marino also has many of the splendid personality traits that Unitas had.

Chuck Crummie, one of Marino's freshman football coaches at Pittsburgh's Central Catholic High School, said:

Danny always had a smile on his face. He was always very congenial, and he got along with people so well. You could see he was a born leader. People followed him; they wanted to be around him, and he made people feel good about themselves through him feeling good about himself. He was a very mature kid.

He wasn't one of those big-time athletes who wouldn't say hello to you or wouldn't be involved in things in school. He was one of the regular guys. I attribute that to his dad, because his dad was a great guy, and I know the two of them were very close.

Often times, when asked who his best coach was, he refers back to his dad. The apple doesn't fall far from the tree. His dad was a great guy, who would do anything for anybody; he would help you out. If something needed done, he was the first one there. I think probably the big thing he taught his son was about humility and how to win graciously, how to accept losing as a part of the learning curve.

Mike Gallagher, who was Marino's video biographer for the Pro Football Hall of Fame, observed: "His dad had unbelievable wisdom. He was very good at knowing what was real in life and what wasn't. He'd say, 'There are factor people and nonfactor people. You worry about the factor people—your parents, your kids.' He taught his son not to worry about things outside of his control, to not waste his time worrying about them."

Gallagher explained that even the reason Marino chose jersey No. 13 was related to his father, who coached him in Little League: "The jerseys ran 1 through 15. His dad said, 'Because you're my kid, you wait until everybody else picks a number, and you get what's left.' Danny got to the point where he said, 'I'm stuck with 13 all the time, so I guess I just might as well fall in love with it.'"

NFL star Mike Lucci once met Dan's father and said: "You could see the pride he had in Danny, but I'm sure it was vice versa. Danny had the love for his dad and didn't want to ever disappoint him."

Lessons learned from his father, Marino was poised and polished in sports early on. Joe Emanuele, Marino's Central Catholic baseball coach, said that the first time he saw Marino he had been told there was a youth league player he just had to see. "I saw this little kid catching and hitting balls over the centerfield wall. Later I told him, 'I'll see you next year at Central.' He said, 'You can't see me there—I'm only 10 years old.' I had to wait three more years."

While Unitas had sharpened his eye and his arm by throwing footballs through an automobile tire, Marino worked with his father. When his dad wasn't around, the aspiring quarterback fired a football at the stop sign near his childhood row house on Parkview Avenue in his Italian–Irish neighborhood, nestled in the Oakland section of Pittsburgh.

Marino still has a sense of loyalty to the city and an understanding of the importance of his roots. "I was very fortunate," he said, "to grow up in an environment like the city of Pittsburgh and the neighborhood of Oakland, an area that was full of football tradition."

Marino also said that having "a certain upbringing, you have to enjoy the sport. People take it very seriously around here—the game of football in Western Pennsylvania. High school football was a big thing."

Even as a kid, he was well aware of that tradition, one as thick as the smoke that belched out of the steel mills. In fact, his home was a mere 10-minute walk from where he would enjoy many an afternoon of glory, Pitt Stadium.

Emanuele said, "In high school, he starred as a freshman as a pitcher, shortstop, and first baseman, and he was a year younger than many classmates. He had big, strong legs. He didn't have his knees worked on until his sophomore or junior year in college. He never had a baseball injury. I just saw him as a baseball player—I wanted so badly for him to go in baseball, but, hey, it worked out."

One year as a pitcher, the 6'4" Marino—already a first-team Parade All-American in high school football—went 8–0 with a nearly invisible 0.78 ERA, throwing 42 consecutive shutout innings. In 1979, when Marino hit .513 as a senior, his Vikings made it all the way to the state semifinals, and his 12–0 record meant he never lost a varsity game (23–0 overall).

"He didn't have to practice baseball. He could do anything he wanted," Emanuele continued. However, that wasn't the case in football. Marino went out for freshman football, and promptly got lost in the shuffle. Even as a sophomore, he was relegated to the JV team, except for taking about three snaps on the varsity squad. "He didn't do anything in football until his junior year when he started, but he got better and better. In baseball, he could go [straight] home, then go out and hit two, three balls out of the park."

Rich Erdelyi, who was Marino's high school football coach, had a tale much like Emanuele's: "The first time I saw Dan, he was playing for St. Regis, probably in eighth grade. He was the biggest kid on the field, the fastest, and the best—he could do it all, and he was 11 or 12 years old. He could throw the ball. He was a terrific player." Crummie was with Erdelyi that day and thought:

Oh, this kid's the real deal. It was solidified when we started to practice with the freshmen. He had something that you can't coach, you can't teach—he just sorta had it, and that's why I always go back to his dad because he had a lot to do with how he threw the ball, how he knew when to throw the ball, and when to throw the ball away. It came from the way his dad coached him and brought him up as a young man.

Dan's abilities? They were evident when I saw him in eighth grade, and they became more evident when he enrolled here as a freshman. You could see it. They say sometimes [about a young player], "Oh, he might be, he might not be." I didn't think there was a doubt in anybody's eyes that he was going to become a professional athlete. I think the only question was what sport it was going to be in.

Crummie said Marino was savvy enough to call audibles, even as a freshman, and that he was also smart enough to dissect games that were in progress with his coaches. Crummie said Marino, even then "a student of the game," would discuss what plays they had run and comment, "I think so-and-so was open down the field," or, "This might work next time." Crummie believes Marino "saw things differently than most people saw them." He concluded, "We coaches knew where we wanted the ball, and that was in his hands."

Erdelyi continued: "Throughout high school he elevated everybody else around him. One of the great games, we beat North Allegheny, 19–18, and that put us in the playoffs. Danny threw three touchdown passes and kicked the extra point to win the game. He kicked off for us, he punted. I didn't let him play defense, but he could have probably done well as a safety man. Dan worked as hard as anybody ever did at practice, and he had a great will to win and to do the best he could at all times. He got mad at practice when he'd throw an incomplete pass."

Crummie said he had great appreciation for the way "Dan orchestrated the game, like it would be a consistent number of passes right on the money that somebody would not have a choice to either catch or miss—I mean they *were* going to catch them. And it was usually in succession. It would be a short pass, followed by another short pass, and then a long one. I think the precision—you looked at him almost like a doctor, the way he operated."

When Marino was about to enter his senior season, he and about five other starters went to see the musical group Boston perform in concert, brushing off a workout and ruining it by their absence. When Erdelyi confronted Marino, he confessed, "We went to a Boston concert."

Erdelyi thought he said he went *to Boston* for a concert and scoffed, "Are you kidding? You've never been out of the North Side of Pittsburgh. You didn't go to Boston for a concert." And he kinda looked at me and said, 'Coach, *Boston*'s a name of a group.'" Erdelyi shook it off, but after the workout he "ran their tails off and made all the other kids stand there and watch. And they're saying, 'He's killing these guys and they're stars. Just think what he's going to do to us if we screw up!' But after that, nobody missed anything."

Coming off a 4–4 season, the Vikings went 9–2 in Marino's senior year. One loss came on a freak late touchdown, and the other came in the opening round of the Western Pennsylvania Interscholastic Athletic League playoffs versus Penn Hills. "He took losses tough," said Erdelyi. "If you talk to Don Shula, he'll tell you the same thing. He didn't want it to be on him."

Although physically mismatched against Penn Hills, Marino's play enabled Central to compete, and Crummie noted, "They say one guy is not going to make a difference, but I think he is one of those kind of athletes that does make that kind of difference."

Although Marino put up very good stats, some critics carped, saying some of his numbers were low. His totals read: 81-for-161 for 1,080 yards and 10 scores as a junior, and 60 of 173 for 1,596 yards and 16 TDs as a senior. Erdelyi elaborated: "Some people say, 'Didn't he throw for, like, 3,000 yards in school?' Nobody threw for that kind of yardage back then. It was a different game." Sometimes he threw as few as a dozen times but, if Central trailed, he might throw the ball 35 times. Other times a pass play was called but, when the defenses sagged, Marino took off running. "Back then, if you threw 15 or 20 passes a game, that was half the game because the clock ran all the time because most people ran the ball."

Marino's team did have a strong running game; however, as Erdelyi noted, even if Marino threw two straight incompletions, "he was never going to be worse than one out of three—so we could throw it every down if we wanted to. And Danny could really run before any knee injuries." Erdelyi estimated Marino's senior rushing yardage at 600–700.

Rich Lackner, Carnegie Mellon University's football coach for 29 years, said Marino was the prototypical quarterback. "In high school, Dan Marino was an incredibly gifted athlete. He had great wheels. It wasn't until some of his injuries caused him to not be as mobile." One of Marino's high school coaches once told Lackner that, when he fired a football, it "rotated so fast that if it went by your ear it would whistle, that's how fast the ball would rotate."

Jeff Petrucci, a coach at the high school and college levels for more than 30 years, once coached Marino for a week in preparation for a high school All-Star game. Petrucci recalled Marino being much like another quarterback he had coached, Joe Montana. They had "physical skills so far superior to all the people around him, it was like a red light where everybody else was a white light kind of thing—he stood out, he was that good."

For example, there was another quarterback working out for the same All-Star game who was headed for Tulane University. Petrucci said, "Danny was so much better than this kid, it was like an eighth grader playing against a high school senior. The [difference] in skill level was so much, you just couldn't imagine it."

Petrucci continued: "Danny was very athletic at that time—he could run like Joe Montana could. Later in his life he had knee injuries and problems. He had a stronger arm than Joe, and he was a great athlete, very skilled." His arm, in fact, was so strong that the Kansas City Royals drafted him out of high school as a pitcher (the same year John Elway was also drafted by the Royals).

Marino decided to play his college ball in his hometown, and the Pitt Panthers were delighted to have him. Who wouldn't welcome a kid who became a 1981 All-American and who shattered school records with ease?

University of Pittsburgh tight end John Brown immediately saw greatness in Marino: "You could see Danny fade back as a freshman, drop back and throw the ball, and the way he threw it, you could tell he was great. If you had to throw the ball through the air 70 yards down the field and try to get a guy, he could do it. If you have to thread the needle and pick up a first down in a, say, big third-and-eight situation, he could do it. There's nobody throws the football on earth better than he does."

Marino, who took Pitt to bowl games in all four of his seasons there, was obviously special. Petrucci said, "He had a presence about him that the great players have, and everybody revolves around those kind of players."

Pitt head coach Jackie Sherrill once asked Marino who had taught him to throw the football the way he did and was informed his father had. Sherrill said, "I told him to never let anyone fool around with his motion, or attempt to change it."

Sherrill called Marino the most focused player he ever had coached. "We'd come out of the tunnel at Pitt Stadium, and everyone was looking at the students in the stands, checking out the crowd, the cheerleaders, you name it. Not Dan. . . . He was thinking about what he had to do, how we were going to win the game."

Let one of Marino's college games serve as an example of his confidence, his focus, and his ability to almost single-handedly cause his team to display great resiliency. That showcase game was his Sugar Bowl performance in his junior season, in which Marino and Pittsburgh trailed the University of Georgia, not once or twice, but three times, and still overcame the deficits.

Vince Dooley, the coach of the Bulldogs in that contest, once won a national title, but he also experienced some bitter defeats along the way. He recalled the time he "had a personal experience with Dan Marino":

> We played Pittsburgh in the Sugar Bowl, and they were up on us, but we finally caught them and went ahead. Then Marino took Pittsburgh down the field. We came down to [very little time] left on the clock. It was fourth-and-five. Pitt called time out, and we decided to blitz Marino, go after him. Their halfbacks picked it up, and it gave him that extra split second to spot the tight end who ran a post, and Marino hit him in the chest. Just as he hit him, our safety man and cornerback hit the tight end. It had to be a perfect pass. Our two guys really hit him hard, but he held on to the ball. I can still see Marino go down to his knees with exultation at that particular moment, and that's my first-hand experience with him.

I keep getting reminded because people keep asking me periodically, about every day: fourth-and-five, same situation—would you blitz? And I tell them, "Hell, no. I know how that came out—I wouldn't do that again. I'd be a fool."

Marino agreed, "The crazy thing about it was Vince Dooley's the coach . . . it's fourth and five and they tried to blitz, and they left one-on-one coverage on John Brown going straight down the middle of the field, and that was kind of a mistake."

When asked if he had other recollections of Marino, Dooley replied, "No. That's enough. I don't want to remember that thing again."

Unlike Dooley, Marino, who in his first three seasons at Pitt helped the Panthers to a 30–3 record, naturally still relishes that comeback victory, and he can still recount the game's closing moments vividly and with alacrity. It was on January 1, 1982, that Pitt and Georgia clashed in that Sugar Bowl. Pitt was down, 20–17, with 42 seconds left to play, and they faced the previously mentioned fourth-down-and-five situation from the 33-yard line. A game-tying field goal was certainly feasible, a viable option, but not in Marino's mind.

Marino picks up the account from the moment when Sherrill called him over to the sidelines. "I think he wanted to kick the field goal, and I said, 'You know, we didn't come here [to play for a tie].' And I wasn't the only one standing there that felt that way."

Sherrill recalled that moment, when Marino said playing for a tie was far from what he had in mind: "Danny looked me in the eye. . . . I knew right then that he would get it done."

Coincidentally, just one day prior to winning the Sugar Bowl, Marino had flatly stated that, as far as he was concerned, "If there is any time at all on the clock, then there is enough time for us to win." That credo stuck with him over his entire career.

Later on, in NFL regular-season play, Marino engineered fourth-quarter or overtime drives to give the Dolphins a lead that they eventually turned into victory 51 times (based on stats dating back to 1960)—more than Brett Favre, more than John Elway, more, in fact, than any pro quarterback ever, through 2016, with the exception of Peyton Manning. Marino came up with such dramatic drives six times in 1985, and six times again some seven years later. Those totals still rank 15th best on that all-time list.

Simply put, Marino exuded confidence. "There are times on the field," he said, as quoted by Dave McMahon, "when I feel like I can't miss, when I'm in complete control and everything just clicks. The ball is always on time, it's always catchable, and I'm making the right decisions on who to throw to. Those are the times when I want to pass on every play because I feel like we're unstoppable."

Crummie agreed, saying that when he observed Marino play high school football, he never saw him, "nervous, under duress, even when he was in a situation where maybe he should have been a little nervous or hurried. He always seemed to have that little bit of extra confidence, and he could hold the ball to the very last minute and not get into too much trouble. He always had that confidence and that savvy that you can't really teach. He had that in high school, in his freshman year and I thought when you watched him play as a pro, he never had that look that he was bothered. He just had that confident look about him."

When Marino left Pitt, he held nearly every school passing record, including the most touchdown passes in a season (37) and the most TD strikes for a career (79). He was more than prepared for life in the pros.

Nevertheless, Marino wasn't selected in the 1983 draft until the 27th pick, due to false rumors of his using drugs. Five other quarterbacks—admittedly some of them standouts like John Elway and Jim Kelly—were chosen ahead of Marino. One Pittsburgh Steelers scout said a rap against Marino was his small hands, a comment that now seems nitpicky, short-sighted, and just plain wrong. Further, the Steelers felt they were still set at quarterback with Marino's childhood idol, Terry Bradshaw, entrenched at that position. Again, they were wrong.

Sherrill felt Marino had it tough at first in Miami, but he persevered and won people over. "The expectations were great for Dan, right from the start. The media in Miami set him up to fail, saying he was the best quarterback since Y. A. Tittle and Johnny Unitas, stuff like that. . . . But he grew up fast, and he's been a real success story." So successful, in fact, he's now held in far higher esteem than Tittle, and he even surpassed Unitas in myriad categories.

In fact, Marino ranks as the 10th greatest NFL player ever on a list by pro-football-reference.com, which evaluates the "approximate value" of players. That statistic attempts to measure how valuable every player was compared to every other player in the NFL from 1950 on.

"When he went to the pros," stated Sherrill, "he went to the best place. Don Shula could see right away that he was something special, and gave him early opportunities to play. He couldn't have been in a better situation."

Armed with talent and a growing faith in himself, Marino became the Miami starting quarterback in his rookie season, "and for the next seventeen years the fortunes of the franchise rode on his shoulders."

He later admitted that, in his first start back in 1983 versus the Buffalo Bills, he was quite nervous. He was standing on the sidelines, when veteran safety Lyle Blackwood approached him. "He came up to me with a serious look and he shook my hand and he said, 'Dan, good luck today. And I don't want you to feel any pressure, but remember one thing: if you play bad, we'll lose.' Now *that's* pressure on a rookie."

Pressure aside, Marino quickly took his team to the playoffs, where he hit 60 percent of his passes while benefiting from the experience of playing in the postseason, albeit in a loss to the Seattle Seahawks.

In 1984, in his first full season (he started in just nine games in 1983), Marino won league MVP honors, and records tumbled like dominos. His stats were of cosmic proportions as he threw for an NFL record 5,084 yards (still the 17th best total ever, through 2016), and his average air yardage per game, a personal best of 317.8 that season, led the league and still ranks No. 10 all-time. His 48 TD throws also set a new pro football mark and remains the fourth highest total ever, absolutely obliterating the old record of 36 set by Blanda in 1961. It took 15 years before another quarterback reached the 40 plateau (Kurt Warner). Marino's quarterback rating glistened at 108.9, and he completed 362 of his 564 passes—and, remember, all this came in his second NFL season and his *first* year as a full-time starter. Further, the 44 touchdowns he threw two years later still rank No. 7 all-time. Overall in 1984, he established six passing records.

In short, his sole MVP season was one of the greatest ever by a quarterback, even though opposing teams tried many schemes to thwart him, including dropping eight men to pass defend.

He steered Miami to a 14–2 record and a trip to the Super Bowl, where, despite Marino's completing 29 of his 50 passes for 318 yards and a touchdown, the Dolphins floundered, losing to Montana and the 49ers, 38–16, in Marino's only Super Bowl appearance.

Lucci commented: "For somebody to say Marino never won a Super Bowl and that's the second thing out of their mouth, they're ignorant.

After a while you say, 'You don't know the price somebody paid to get there, and he had great success.' He was a great football player and I'm sure Dan doesn't wake up in the morning thinking, 'Shit, I didn't win the Super Bowl.' It almost becomes a joke that such great football players are being measured by something [unfairly]. It's a team sport."

There can be no question that Marino's teammates were a boon to his career as he normally enjoyed great pass protection. In 1988, he was sacked a record low 0.98 percent of the time (only six sacks, despite his throwing the ball 606 times); the following season, the rate of 1.79 still stands No. 9 on that list. In fact, on the list of the top 21 seasons based on this stat for regular season quarterback protection, Marino's name appears five times. For a career, no quarterback ever enjoyed better protection based on this stat—Marino and Peyton Manning are tied at a sack percentage rate of 3.13 percent. As a matter of fact, Marino led the NFL in this area 10 times, including every season from 1983, his rookie year, through 1989.

Sportscaster Mike Gallagher said: "Danny was the spokesperson for Isotoner [gloves], and one of the commercials was, 'Protect the hands that protect you,' and he took it seriously, got them gloves and took care of them. Even at Pitt his best friends were Jimbo Covert, Emil Boures, Russ Grimm, and Paul Dunn, who were all [offensive] linemen."

On occasions when the defense did get to Marino, Tom Matte said he was so strong that sometimes "guys would bounce off of him—great competitor. Shula really made the most out of him."

While there were no more trips to the Super Bowl for Marino, his accomplishments were legion. In 1985, he guided a 12–4 team, his last playoff-caliber team until 1990; in 1986, he again led the NFL in completions. That season, for the third season running, he also threw for the most touchdowns.

The 1987 through 1989 seasons were rather bleak record-wise for Marino as Miami's starting quarterback, at 7–5, 6–10, and 8–8, respectively, but for the most part he rolled on. In 1988, he again led the league in competitions and yards passing, and he repeated that performance in 1992.

In 1994, Miami went 10–6 and won the Wild Card playoff game over Montana and the Kansas City Chiefs. In that game, both Montana and Marino tossed two TDs, and Marino went 26-of-37 for 314 yards. In the Dolphins' next game, versus the Chargers, Marino chalked up three first-half touchdowns, but his 21–6 lead slipped away, and San Diego eliminated Miami.

Despite Marino's 422 yards through the air on 64 attempts in Miami's only 1995 playoff game, Buffalo prevailed, 37–22, in a Jim Kelly–Dan Marino showdown.

In 1997, Marino led the NFL for the last time in a major category, with 319 completions. He followed that up with another 10–6 record in 1998, the year he hit on almost 70 percent of his passes in two playoff games; however, he suffered through a sub-.500 record (5–6) as a starter the next season, dashing forever his hopes to revisit the Super Bowl.

Scott Zolak finished his eight-year career in 1999 as one of three quarterbacks for Miami. There he had the opportunity to play with, observe, and become acquainted with Marino. "He was an idol of mine. To spend his last year, which was also my last year, together was pretty cool."

As Zolak got to know Marino, the image of his idol was not, as often happens, tarnished:

Danny was always holding court at his locker, and he always had us over to his house in Weston, outside of Fort Lauderdale after games. It was almost like you're down at the local Moose lodge or local VFW. He would put on a spread. He'd just dump out these bushels of stone crabs on top of his table outside, and [provide] all you can drink.

Danny had this massive trophy-case room with a wine cellar attached to it in his house. It had multi-thousand dollar bottles of wine, but we would never drink the good stuff. All of us guys from Pittsburgh would always break out this stuff from a Mason jar—Danny had this stuff called Uncle Chuckie's Homemade Wine that one of his uncles back in Pittsburgh made. We ended up drinking at his house all night. I think it was close to moonshine, but that's the stuff we appreciated, that homemade stuff. Or somebody would send halupkis down to us. When you make it with your hands, not buy it in the store, the prepackaged cases, it means something.

Gallagher observed, "Danny always remembered Western Pennsylvania, remembered home." He once needed to ask Marino about something, but not wishing to bother him several days away from game time, Gallagher decided to approach Dan's father instead. When Dan learned of this he told Gallagher, "Well the day that I can't talk to you three days before a game, is the day I should quit."

Zolak remembered, "Danny was really good at taking care of the guys on the team. He loved being around the guys, loved being one of the guys."

Able to blend in off the field, Marino stood out and was dead serious when it came to football. Zolak continued: "Danny had such great competitiveness, and he had a bad rap for chewing out guys, but he was so intense. Such an intense player. He always demanded your best. He was great to be around."

Zolak said Marino was "a lot like Bill Parcells—they chewed people out, man. They would keep you on your toes. Danny was really good at busting balls." In other words, Marino, a veritable head coach on the field, was a take-charge leader who, true to his roots, took full responsibility for his actions while expecting his troops to also live up to their roles as professionals.

Lucci added, "You look at people you enjoy being around. You look at Marino, you look at Kelly, you look at Namath, they had charisma. It's like people responded to them. They had the talent, but they also have the charisma and the ability to pull people together."

The year Pitt went to the Sugar Bowl in New Orleans, the school's budget would not permit the dozen or so equipment managers to make the trip. One of them was Mike Gallagher, who recalled: "Danny went up to the head coach and said, 'These guys work practice everyday. They do everything for us.' Ultimately, they sent everybody because of Danny, and he didn't have to care about us, but he genuinely did."

Bimbo Cecconi, a member of the All-Time Pitt Team, has seen a lot of quarterbacks over his 80-plus years of living. He felt a lot of the qualities many great quarterbacks share such as leadership were "just born in them. You got guys like Dan Marino and his great release. With that, he also had a great mind, and he knew the game. And he was tall and strong." In many ways, then, Marino was the total package.

Scott Zolak appreciated Marino's "from-the-chest release, the quickness, the snap of the wrist." He said:

> I've been around a lot of guys that stand there and throw balls, but the rotation on his football was more than any other guy I remember. I mean, Elway can throw it through a wall, Kelly can throw it hard, but I thought Marino had that quick pocket release, right from the chest. And his competitive nature was like no other one I've ever seen.
>
> I've been around Drew Bledsoe a long time. If Drew had some of what Danny had, and that's no disrespect to Drew—he competed—but

he was more of an even-keel guy. Danny was a fire-and-brimstone, rip-your-ass type guy. He would get in guys' faces, but he wasn't showing guys up. A lot of people think he always showed his receivers up, but when you're around him it comes across as his competitive nature.

Fred Cox said Marino was much like the rest of the quarterbacks out of the Pittsburgh area as far as his background went; however, speaking of The Six, he said, "There's no question Marino had the quickest release and a strong arm. Jim Kelly had a really strong arm, but I don't think his arm was nearly as quick as Marino's."

Ditka added, "You can have a quick release, but you gotta be smart, and he was." Ditka said Marino's release was a matter of "anticipation. With the great quarterbacks, you can't throw the ball where the receiver is, you gotta throw it where he's going to be, and that's what he had—a lot of that. He made the weapons around him great; they didn't make him great. He was smart."

Smart and crafty. In a 1994 contest, the Jets led Miami by three with around 30 seconds to play, and the Dolphins were eight yards away from a touchdown. With no time-outs left, Marino signaled he was going to spike the ball to kill the clock. Like a smooth con man, his action was just a ploy. He took the snap and hit Mark Ingram for the game-winning strike.

Allan Maki chipped in on the motif of Marino's release. "He delivered the ball crisply—like the snap of a wet towel being cracked in the wind—with the precision of a watchmaker's hand: quite simply, a thing of beauty." Maki felt that Marino "redefined the position, taking what quarterback Dan Fouts and Air Coryell had in San Diego and expanding on the premise that the best, quickest way to move the football was by throwing it."

Maki also noted that putting the ball up often meant occasional interceptions, but that "didn't faze him. He never shied away from a mistake. Caution was for losers. Marino kept throwing the ball, undeterred until he finally rammed it down your throat."

One opponent, star defensive back Ronnie Lott, conceded: "You were basically at Dan's mercy. All the great ones see the game so quickly that when everybody else is running around like a chicken with his head cut off, they know exactly where they want to go with the ball. It's like they see everything in slow motion."

Marino responded admirably to the pressure, largely due to his tools and his faith in them. Former Baltimore Colt Sam Havrilak said Marino had "probably the best release of any quarterback I've ever seen, and he had an extremely strong arm. He wasn't very fast or agile in the pocket, but he could pick apart a defense because of his arm strength and ability to read defenses."

Comparisons with other quarterbacks are, of course, inevitable. As Dooley put it, Marino "was a pretty good-sized guy—the first of those big quarterbacks, I guess." He said Marino may not have had "the mobility of, say, an Archie Manning," but, more to the point, Dooley was cognizant of Marino's overall ability; when he had to oppose him in the Sugar Bowl, it was intimidating. "Yeah," said Dooley. "That's the problem. That firearm passing. He probably could put the ball in a spot better than anybody." Of The Six, Marino is Dooley's pick for possessing the strongest arm, one that enabled him to laser beam his passes right on the button.

Pittsburgh sportswriter Chuck Finder compared Marino with Montana, liking both, but pointing out:

> You still find people who argue about those guys being in the top five quarterbacks of all-time. I don't think anybody would ever throw Marino out of the top five—they might Montana because Marino threw for more yardage and was more of a pure passer, whereas Steve Young followed Montana and took off some of the luster of Joe's NFL accomplishments because it appeared to be Bill Walsh and the system as much as Joe Montana.
>
> How many times Marino threw for 400 yards when that was not done in those days—nobody else did it. Today we see quarterbacks do it on occasion, but Marino did it every darn week, 300, 400, 500 yards.

He still has the record for most 400-yard games with 13, almost exactly double the output of the men tied for No. 2 in this category through 2016—Montana, Warren Moon, and Peyton Manning (7 such games each).

Indeed, week in and week out, Marino was firing away for an NFL eternity. Marino left the game after playing in 242 games, more than nearly every other quarterback ever. He held 19 NFL records and shared five more. With all that he accomplished, a line from Shakespeare about Julius Caesar seems to apply to Marino: "Here was a Caesar! When comes such another?"

JIM KELLY

The Linebacker-Tough Quarterback

7

Select lifetime facts, statistics, and records of note: Kelly was so adept at leading late game-winning drives that he is ranked No. 20 all-time with 29 in that department as of the end of the 2016 season. His average yards thrown per game was 221.7, good enough to register as the 33rd best ever. As for his grand total of 35,467 yards passing, that stands as the 25th highest mark ever in NFL action. He's 21st on the list for the most net yards gained per pass attempt, at almost exactly six-and-a-half yards per pop. Toss in his 84.4 career quarterback rating, and he cracks the top 40 all-time at No. 37. He fired 237 touchdowns, 27th best ever, and until just recently he was in the top 25 for passes attempted and passes completed.

A five-time Pro Bowler, Jim Kelly was in the top 10 nearly every season for every passing statistic that exists. That even includes such seldom-cited categories such as longest passes of the season, lowest percentage of his throws intercepted, and net yards gained per pass attempts. In 1988 and again in 1993, he led the NFL in game-winning drives and comeback wins. He hit on just a smidge over 60 percent of his passes lifetime during his prodigious 11-year career.

• • •

There's no getting around it. Any discussion of Jim Kelly seems to begin with and often focuses on his 0–4 record in Super Bowl play, even though that is patently unfair.

It is unfortunate that, of The Six, only Kelly lacks a monumental defining moment (or moments) in his career. Blanda had his remarkable run of comeback victories as a geriatric whiz. Unitas is best remembered for his win in what is still frequently referred to as The Greatest Game Ever Played. Namath had his Ruthian "called shot" of a win in Super Bowl III. Montana had more than his share of moments, but going with his three

Super Bowl MVP showings should suffice. Perhaps Marino's great comeback in his Sugar Bowl win over Georgia can serve for his best moment of glory—or consider the many NFL records he set as a body of work.

Unfortunately for Kelly, most fans remember that, yes, he took the Buffalo Bills to eight postseason appearances, but his teams lost four Super Bowls. They somehow neglect to praise and respect him for getting his Bills that far for such a long stretch of excellence. After all, every year a slew of teams would be delighted to make it to the ultimate game, and the strong-armed Kelly became the first quarterback ever to steer his team to four *consecutive* Super Bowls.

That his Bills don't get significant credit for such success irks Kelly, who notes that his peers, such as Elway and Marino, are "amazed at how we were able to do that."

Remember this, too: Kelly would have won at least one Super Bowl had things gone just a bit differently. In the opening round of the 1990 playoffs, he contributed three touchdown passes and led the Bills to a 44-point explosion versus Miami. Then Kelly set an AFC title game record by completing 73.9 percent of his passes as Buffalo took apart the Los Angeles Raiders, 51–3, even though the Raiders had given up the second lowest point total in their conference. The Bills advanced to play the New York Giants in Super Bowl XXV, a game that wasn't decided until the last seconds of the final quarter.

To his credit, Kelly had to engineer the Bills' final drive by taking charge, down by a single point, at his own 10-yard line with 2:16 to go. With time almost expiring, and after marching his team 51 yards in two minutes and eight seconds, Kelly gave way to the kicking unit. Scott Norwood then missed the infamous "wide right" field goal attempt from 47 yards out. The football tailed late in its flight and sailed about two feet wide of the uprights, and the Giants prevailed, 20–19. During the regular season, Norwood had successfully booted 6 out of 10 field goals from 40–49 yards out.

Kelly threw for 212 yards, hitting on 60 percent of his passes that day. Later he stated quite philosophically, "The Super Bowl is supposed to come down to the last kick. If you want to write a script of the game, this is what you have to write." He fully realized he and his Bills had battled bravely, and that sometimes even great teams fall short. Again, Super Bowl defeats should not automatically diminish a team or a player's prowess.

Statistically speaking, especially considering that quarterbacks face stronger defenses in the postseason than they do in the regular season as a rule, Kelly threw as well or better in playoff action as in regular season play. That fact tends to dismiss charges that he didn't play well in big games—a view sometimes advanced for why his Bills lost Super Bowls.

Consider the numbers. In regular season action, Kelly hit on 60 percent of his passes, compared to 59 percent in postseason contests. Rounded off, his rate of passes intercepted was identical (5 percent, regardless of what type of game he was involved in); he even threw for slightly more yards per game in the playoffs, 227 to 222. His regular season stats involving average touchdowns per game does hold a 1.48 to 1.23 edge over playoff contests; again, that differential isn't huge, and it does reflect the fact that the defenses one faces tend to be much tougher in postseason competition than during regular season play.

Nevertheless, there was little consolation for Kelly, who stated that "the problem with losing a Super Bowl is that, after all the hard work you put into getting there, you suddenly find that you have to start all over to get there again."

Kelly carries the agony of not winning it all. "I know the losses in the Super Bowl killed him," said Kelly's high school coach, Terry Henry, "but on the outside you wouldn't know it."

Perhaps his upbringing in East Brady explains his stoicism in the face of harrowing defeats. Kelly, who repeatedly expressed his pride over representing his small hometown, was well aware that the local coal mines had been shut down for quite some time, so he began to strive to make a good life for himself. His family, he wrote in his autobiography *Armed and Dangerous,* had to "scratch and claw for everything we had," and some of their meals "consisted of baked beans, period." On some occasions, he stated, he would go the entire day with just a peanut-butter-and-jelly sandwich for nourishment. Some years the children received little else beyond a shirt and one pair of pants.

Kelly's father, Joe, who had been raised in an orphanage since he was two years old, was a machinist. Author Tom Callahan quoted Jim Kelly as saying his father had "those rough, sandpaper hands" associated with a man accustomed to hard work. His mother worked at stretching each paycheck that was brought into the household of six children, all boys. To their credit, the boys took jobs to help out as well.

His mother taught Jim to be kind to disadvantaged people. Coach Henry said: "She worked in the cafeteria at the school. Sometimes she threw an extra bigger scoop for some of those kids that she knew might not be getting a meal at home."

Kelly's father had only a passing interest in team sports, but he learned everything he could about them in order to help his sons. He also taught his boys to be tough. If two of them got into a fight, Joe made them put on boxing gloves and football helmets and then, as Kelly wrote, "let us pound the crap out of each other."

Kelly and his brothers loved to play football so much they played indoors with the three oldest brothers acting like the defensive line and the three other brothers serving as running backs attempting to plunge through the line. They even wore helmets, but many "bumps, bruises, bloody noses, broken bones, and concussions" still occurred.

Kelly honed his throwing skills by competing with friends to see who could throw stones the farthest, taking aim across the Allegheny River.

Kelly began his organized football days when he was eight, playing midget football as a tight end. The next year, the coach made him the quarterback, and from that moment on he relished being in control of the offense.

Early on, Joe taught his son that one can't always win, saying almost prophetically "that sooner or later, you'll go up against somebody better than you." Joe also coached his son with intensity, stressing being able to throw a variety of passes without even thinking about that task. He prepared Jim for his first Punt, Pass & Kick (PP&K) competition, working him hard even during Jim's 45-minute lunch breaks from school. "Someday you're going to thank me for this," he told Jim, again with a sense of precognition. "If you want something bad enough, you have to work for it."

He was correct on both counts. In 1970, when Jim was 10 years old, he made it to the national semifinals of the Punt, Pass & Kick competition. The next year he won his second-straight area PP&K title at Three Rivers Stadium. There, he got to meet Terry Bradshaw, and told him, "I am going to take your job away, Mr. Bradshaw."

Jim Kelly's high school coach, Terry Henry, remembered:

When I got the head football coaching job at East Brady, Jim was a youngster playing in the midget football program, and at that time he was the largest one on the team, 5'11". You sort of knew he had a special ability. I coached his brother Raymond, who was my quarterback when Jim was in ninth grade. If Jim could have played when he was in ninth grade, he would have, but the rules did not allow it.

So I waited until his sophomore year to get him. We lost three games that year and didn't lose another game after that. We were in a small league, but we were successful and that got him to be a little bit recognized—in Pennsylvania we were No. 1 his senior year.

When Jim's brother Pat was drafted by the Colts, it provided Jim with inspiration and a reaffirmation that his father's coaching truly paid off. Each of the six Kelly boys played high school football for the East Brady Bulldogs.

There were just 23 boys on the high school squad, and Jim wound up playing quarterback, punter, placekicker, linebacker, defensive end, and safety. His quarterbacking days began as a sophomore, when he took the team to a 7–3 slate, throwing for 1,108 yards and 14 touchdowns. Terry Henry stated, "His senior year, he probably played half of the games because we would be so far ahead at half time that you'd let him start the third quarter then you'd pull him out."

Actually, Kelly got more excited about making a hard hit than throwing a touchdown pass. The next year, the team went undefeated: he completed 58 percent of his passes, and threw for nearly 1,500 yards. He enjoyed another undefeated season the next year, when he hit on 63 percent of his throws. Overall, his record at quarterback was 26–3–1, and he threw for 3,915 yards and 44 touchdowns.

Henry said, "Jim made the Big 33 [squad], something we never had at East Brady High School, and participated in the Big 33 game." As a matter of fact, almost every great quarterback out of Western Pennsylvania played in that showcase contest, including Namath, Montana, Marino, and Bulger. At least one player from each of the first 43 Super Bowls also played in the Big 33 Football Classic, an event that dates back to 1957—more proof Western Pennsylvania deserves the title of football factory.

As a basketball player, Kelly helped his team make the state quarterfinals as a junior and the semifinals as a senior. He was the first player from his school to score 1,000 points and grab 1,000 rebounds in his career. As a 6'3", 195-pound senior, he was good for 23 points and 20 rebounds per game.

Kelly once wrote that he grew up watching Bradshaw and Namath and dreamed of being in a Steelers uniform himself, even though he came from a town of around 1,000 people. He wondered how a kid from a small Irish Catholic community could ever get noticed. After all, his hometown was nearly invisible, a pinprick on a map and a town so removed from the mainstream that the nearest McDonald's was a 30-mile drive away.

Despite all that, Kelly did envision that he would somehow become a success. In fifth grade, he drew a picture, signed it, and gave it to a girl he was trying to impress. He told her the autograph would be worth money someday because he was going to be a pro quarterback, another Bradshaw.

His high school feats led to a few, then a slew, of colleges recruiting him—especially schools, said Henry, "from the eastern part of the United States coming after him."

It would have made sense for Kelly to stay in state and go to Pitt or Penn State. He was very loyal to his hometown, even referring to his family as the East Brady Bunch in his autobiography.

Henry stated: "He wanted to go to Penn State in the worst way—he went to their football camp two years in a row, but when J. T. White came to recruit him, he was up front and said, 'Jim, we're recruiting you for linebacker.' I was shocked, and Jim knew immediately that he did not want to go to Penn State. He wanted to be a quarterback. It was a $40,000 scholarship, but he said no."

At that point, according to Henry, "the Pitts, the Marylands, the West Virginias, the Miamis, the other schools started recruiting him a little heavier."

Deciding not to become another player to travel the well-trod path from Western Pennsylvania to Notre Dame, Kelly narrowed his options down to Tennessee and Miami, even though that school had enjoyed just one winning season over the last nine years and home game attendance had plummeted to around 20,000 fans per game.

Henry said: "I think he looked at Miami as having more of an open program. He thought he could go in there and possibly play. Lou Saban was the coach at the time, and they guaranteed us they were going to do a straight drop-back passing game, but when [Kelly] got there they were running the veer offense, which we did in high school. Jim was more of a straight drop-back passing quarterback, and he proved that at Miami and in the NFL.

"When Saban left, they brought in Howard Schnellenberger, and he brought in Earl Morrall [to work with the passing game], and that was the change in Jim's game."

Schnellenberger turned things around drastically. He had coached quarterbacks such as Bob Griese and Morrall with the Dolphins and Namath and Stabler at Alabama. Kelly called Schnellenberger's decison to bring Morrall in to tutor him "the best thing that could have ever happened to my football career."

In 1979, Kelly took over for good as the Miami quarterback in his second year (after being redshirted). His ascension to the starter's role came during the seventh game of the season, when Syracuse was blowing them out. That game, coincidentally, was played at the site of Kelly's future NFL home, Rich Stadium.

His first start came at Penn State. Miami was approximately a 30-point underdog, but Kelly threw a 57-yard touchdown pass on the first play of the game, and Miami went on to win, 26–10, even though Kelly's jaw was dislocated—also on the game's first play.

Kelly felt vindicated, and showed Penn State's head coach Joe Paterno that he was, in fact, a quarterback, not a linebacker. Schnellenberger commented, "I've never seen a quarterback play as well and as poised in his debut as Kelly was today."

Over his first three starts, he suffered the jaw injury, a concussion, and cracked ribs, but like the old slogan for Timex watches, he took a licking and kept on ticking.

In 1980, Miami earned a visit to the Peach Bowl, ending a 13-year dry spell for bowl appearances. They won, 20–10, over Virginia Tech, giving Miami a 9–3 record, their best since 1966.

Highlights of 1981 included a Halloween shocker over No. 1–ranked Penn State and a lopsided win over Notre Dame, only the school's second victory ever over the Fighting Irish. In that game, Kelly broke the school's records for lifetime passing yards and touchdowns. However, due to recruiting violations, there would be no bowl appearance this year, despite their 9–2 record and No. 8 ranking.

Entering his final season, Kelly was praised by Schnellenberger: "I don't think any one kid has meant so much to a program and its turnaround as Jim Kelly. Pitt was good before Dan Marino. So was Georgia before Herschel Walker. Jim's the most productive quarterback I've been around. And that includes Joe Namath and Ken Stabler."

Kelly suffered a total separation of the AC joint of his throwing shoulder in the season's third game. After an operation, he was told his playing days were probably over, but he replied, "I have never quit anything in my life and am not about to start." He found solace in thinking, "You're a Kelly. You're tough, you're a survivor."

He still maintains that attitude. In March 2014, following initial diagnosis and surgery in 2013, his mouth cancer reappeared, and he had to undergo six weeks of aggressive treatment. He revealed that he was in constant pain and had no feeling on the left side of his face. Already his upper jaw and each of his teeth save two had been removed. He had a plate and 6 screws inserted into his neck and two plates and 10 screws in his back. In addition, he once had a cyst under his nostril removed without the benefit of novocaine; in 2010 he was in a plane crash in Alaska that left him swimming in the Bering Sea in 39° waters. He endured, but lost 23 pounds due to the ordeal. Compared to those Job-like tribulations, coming back from the separation of the AC joint was relatively easy.

He ended his college career completing 63 percent of his passes, while setting school records for career passing yards, total yards, completions, and touchdown passes. Despite that, he still had to prove himself to NFL scouts. He did so shortly before the 1983 draft, putting on an impressive show that some called the "Kelly Sweepstakes." The Bills drafted him at No. 14, ahead of future stars such as Marino, but Kelly signed a lucrative contract for the new United States Football League (USFL).

Kelly compared his signing to that of Joe Namath, saying the league felt the need to sign an impact player to give the USFL quick credibility. He wore the uniform of the Houston Gamblers in 1984 and 1985.

Kelly paid immediate dividends, winning the Western Conference championship in his first season. He enjoyed a homecoming that year, leading the Gamblers to a 47–26 win over the Pittsburgh Maulers. East Brady residents packed 12 buses to make the trip to the Steel City to watch the town's most famous native throw for 367 yards and five touchdowns.

Kelly became the 1984 MVP, passing for 5,219 yards and 44 touchdowns, a new professional football record that stood briefly until Marino threw 48 that fall. Kelly's nine games with at least 300 yards passing also established another pro record that Marino tied a few months later.

In 1985, Kelly once threw for 574 yards and five touchdowns and went 120 passes without throwing an interception. He was the top-rated passer; over his two years in the USFL, he threw for more yards and touchdowns than any other quarterback.

Then the league folded, and it was time for Kelly to shuffle off to Buffalo, signing with the Bills as a free agent in 1986, putting his signature on an $8 million contract that instantly made him the highest-paid player in the NFL. He persuaded his father to retire, gave him a credit card, and told him to charge anything at all because he would take care of the bill.

The Bills were coming off back-to-back 2–14 seasons, and the average home attendance had dwindled to 37,000. Coach Marv Levy took over the floundering team after Hank Bullough was dismissed, inheriting a 2–7 record, and things began to change. Buffalo upset the Steelers in Buffalo, before a crowd that included many East Brady natives. Kelly called it one of the most gratifying wins he ever experienced.

Buffalo head coach Marv Levy stated, "Kelly energized the team. Immediately, that vital position was filled by a man whose combination of talent, leadership, toughness, and ability to inspire confidence has rarely been matched."

Levy believed no other quarterback had ever done as well as Kelly in his inaugural NFL season. "He's better as a first-year player than Dan Marino was or Joe Montana or Terry Bradshaw or Johnny Unitas. . . ."

Another change occurred when Buffalo unveiled the no-huddle attack, which they called the "K-Gun," in the first game of 1990, doing so on a limited basis. Rich Erdelyi said that Kelly was perfect for that offense. "He was a quick decision maker, and I think he made correct decisions, and that's what it takes. One, two, three, four, five, throw. You're making your decision on your first step and throwing it on your fifth step."

Writer Hank Hersch labeled Kelly as a "mastermind of the Bills' no-huddle offense, a rat-a-tat attack designed to keep defenses off-balance and unable to shuttle in new personnel to fit the down and distance. With a veteran line, a pair of game breakers in running back Thurman Thomas and wideout Andre Reed and a coolheaded play-caller in Kelly, Buffalo's no-huddle was no-holds-barred."

Kelly, a self-proclaimed perfectionist, once wrote that, when the Bills went to the no-huddle look, he was allowed to call his own plays. That meant a lot to him, knowing Levy trusted him.

That season Levy made the decision to reduce the number of plays they executed out of their no-huddle offense. Now, he pointed out, each play got more repetitions in practice, and "there was no need to slow things down by getting in the quarterback's ear via the headset." The result was that the "swashbuckling [Kelly] loved operating this way. He exuded confidence, and that confidence spilled over onto his teammates."

At the same time, opponents detested defending against Kelly and found they had difficulty trying to shuttle substitutes into games when certain "down and yardage situations" called for such strategic moves.

The Bills excelled because, as Levy observed, the offense had "the threat of the forward pass and because Jim didn't give a damn about his own statistics, [so he] was able to strike the perfect balance between the running and passing games." With runners such as Thurman Thomas, the Bills' offense was, in fact, explosive.

Aside from the Super Bowls, Kelly played in and won many a big game. In January 1991, he took on Marino and the Dolphins with snow and sleet buffeting around the field in Buffalo. The game ended with the highest combined score in a regulation playoff contest. Buffalo racked up nearly 500 yards of offense to the Dolphins' 430, and the 44–34 win propelled the Bills into the AFC championship game for the second time in three years.

For that game, some 80,324 fans packed Orchard Park to see Buffalo defeat the Los Angeles Raiders, despite frostbite-inducing weather. Kelly and company did not disappoint, waltzing to the previously mentioned 51–3 shellacking of the Raiders. Kelly threw for exactly 300 yards and two scores, and the Bills churned out 502 yards. For the first time in franchise history, the Buffalo Bills were headed to the Super Bowl.

Super Bowl XXV, pitting the Bills against the New York Giants, was the one in which a missed field goal cost the Bills a championship, but they had battled valiantly. Five times the lead had changed hands as Thurman Thomas scampered for 135 yards, despite having only 15 carries, and Kelly hit on 60 percent of his passes.

The next season the Bills led the league in total yards and scoring, again with a balanced attack. Levy stated, "He called most of the plays . . . and there has never been a more unselfish signal caller than Jim." When the Bills built up a safe lead, Kelly would run the ball, unworried about padding his stats. However, if a defense geared up for the run so much they became vulnerable to a pass, Kelly would "scorch them in a hurry." Levy also praised Kelly as the best quarterback he ever coached when it came to dealing "with the unexpected or an adverse turn of events."

Kelly had to revel in his 1991 win in Pittsburgh, when he trounced the Steelers, 52–34, throwing six touchdowns in the process. In one 1991 game versus Miami, he hurt an ankle in the third quarter and was told he would sit out the rest of the game. However, he always felt that if he wasn't carried off the field in a given game, he would somehow come back to play. Against Miami, he did just that, leading touchdown marches of 80, 70, and 55 yards.

That season, Super Bowl XXVI pitted the Bills against the Redskins, who owned a 24–0 lead 16 seconds into the third quarter. The Bills and Kelly never gave up. They rallied and cut the 23-point lead to 13, at 37–24. However, Kelly had sustained a mild concussion, his second in a matter of months, halfway through the second quarter. Even though he was hurt, he fought with the trainers to stay in the game. Kelly was not unlike a prizefighter in a daze. As they used to say before the era of political correctness: he was on Queer Street, but still insisted he could fight on. The trainers had to tug at a yelling and swearing Kelly to get him off the field. Shortly after, he returned to the game and threw two touchdown passes despite playing through a haze.

Again, it seems unfair to pin the loss on Kelly: he was sacked five times, knocked down after releasing the ball 10 times, hurried into making 13 bad throws, and experienced 2 balls batted back at him. His protection broke down early and often. In his autobiography, Kelly wrote that he knew that playing quarterback was risky, that "there might as well be a bull's-eye painted on your jersey." He also stated that some of the hits he took were his own fault because of his "constant desire to make the big play. I always want to wait until the last possible second. . . ."

Nearly as stubborn as he is tough, Kelly also said he prides himself on coming back stronger after a hard hit. "I guess I just want to prove to the defense that it takes more than one shot to get me out of there." He added that he would do anything to pick up an extra inch if it meant reaching a first down or plunging into the end zone, "even if it means going helmet to helmet with somebody."

After the Super Bowl loss to Washington, Kelly told the media he wasn't sure what he was about to say would make sense, due to his head injury. He stated he "couldn't remember a whole lot of details from the game. And maybe it was better that way. The part I can remember, I didn't like."

Levy called it a "noble effort," and vowed that the Bills would become the first team to claw back to play in another Super Bowl after losing two in a row.

The Bills' first road game in 1992 featured a crowd-drawing Montana vs. Kelly marquee. Footballs flew all over the place like clay pigeons, and the game ended without either team punting. Kelly helped wrap this one up, 34–31, throwing for more than 400 yards.

In the AFC title game, Miami and Marino were at center stage. While Marino did account for all but 33 of Miami's 276 yards, Kelly adjusted to the Dolphins' attempts to take away what Levy called "our quick-tempo, quick-strike, long-passing game." Instead of trying to force passes against their defense, Kelly threw short stuff (hitting running backs and tight ends on 12-of-17 passes), called for many runs, and generally devoured the clock, keeping the dangerous Marino on the bench in a 29–10 victory.

The loss to Dallas in Super Bowl XXVII cannot be blamed on Kelly, either. Down 14–7, largely due to the Cowboys' converting two turnovers into scores, Kelly suffered a concussion. Dallas won in a 52–17 cakewalk.

The next season Buffalo won 14 games in all and owned the best record in the AFC, defeating all three of the teams who had beaten them in earlier Super Bowls.

In their first postseason game, they trailed Oakland by 11 with a minute left in the first half. Kelly gathered up his teammates and took charge. "If we don't get our butts in gear," he admonished, "we aren't going to win this damn game." Four plays and 76 yards later, the lead had been cut to four.

Entering the fourth quarter, down 23–22, Levy said Kelly again came through, taking the Bills 71 yards in nine plays for a touchdown. After clinging to the lead, they were again headed to their fifth AFC title game in six years after yet another outstanding overall showing by Kelly.

He won that game, yet another win-or-go-home challenge, begging the question, "What more could *rational* critics expect?" This time they toppled the Kansas City Chiefs of Joe Montana and Marcus Allen. Things were tenuous at the end of the third quarter with Buffalo up, 20–13. A Kelly-driven 79-yard march ate up time and led to a field goal, and a final touchdown made it 30–13.

Kelly once commented: "I thrive on having everything put in my hands. I love being the guy who has to get it done. I've always been that way. Little League football, high school football, even high school basketball. Every game just seemed to wind up in my hands—if I made the big play, we were usually very successful; if I didn't, we usually lost. And that's what I like best about the no-huddle offense. Whether we score points or don't score points is in my hand." More often than not, he did put the points up on the board.

A Super Bowl rematch from the year before again resulted in a Dallas win (30–13). Forced to throw often, Kelly fired the football 50 times, hit on 31-for-53 yards more than Dallas quarterback Troy Aikman, but that didn't console Kelly and the Bills.

Kelly played in three more postseason contests, two in 1995, when he was nearing the age of 36, and one in his final season, 1996. That year was one in which Kelly played pretty well despite being plagued by injuries. Levy called him "the toughest SOB to ever take a snap from center," and admired him for enduring, despite "a variety of recurring bumps, bruises, sprains, strains, headaches, and assorted other Tylenol-devouring ailments."

One little-known fact about Kelly is this: 29 times in his career, he mounted a game-winning drive, defined as a fourth-quarter or overtime drive that resulted in the Bills taking a lead that the team then never surrendered. Those key comebacks are only four fewer than Montana, who is probably *the* quarterback whom most fans associate with that ability to drive a team to a late win while overcoming a deficit or a tie.

When he limped away from the game, Kelly had topped the 3,000-yard mark in passing eight times. He led his league in completions (63.3 percent in 1990) and touchdowns thrown (33 in 1991) once; in quarterback rating once (101.2 in 1990); and in percentage of passes attempted that went for touchdowns on two occasions.

However, when Levy introduced Kelly when he was inducted into the Hall of Fame, Levy observed, "Never mind his eye-popping statistics, he never cared about them anyway. He cared about winning, and he was a winner. He cared about his team and about his teammates." A winner indeed—Kelly's regular season record as a starting quarterback stood at 101–59.

Levy added, "Never mind about his arm—it was great—but what was really noteworthy about Jim was his heart. Jim Kelly's heart was about as stout as a nose tackle's butt." Levy then pointed to Kelly's toughness, reminding people how Penn State coach Joe Paterno had tried to recruit Kelly to play linebacker at the school known as "Linebacker U."

Sam Havrilak evaluated Kelly by saying, "He had a strong arm, not as strong as Marino, but I would consider Jim Kelly more of a natural leader than Marino. I think his players rallied around him a lot more than they did around Marino."

Mike Lucci said: "Everybody that I talked to, players from Buffalo and their coach, said that Kelly was a great uniter. He pulled everybody together. They had great respect for each other, almost a love for each other. And [his teammates] believed that he was going to get them to go. They responded well to him."

Terry Henry also saw Kelly as a leader his team stood behind and said that after each of Kelly's NFL games, "win or lose in Buffalo, he would have a party at his house. Talk about a team player—he would have a caterer come in and everybody would stay until 2, 3, 4:00 in the morning after not getting there until 7 or 8:00. It would be nothing to see Thurman Thomas bartending. When we went through the years, Jim would hire bartenders to come in. You might have 100, 150 people in his basement. It kind of pulled the team together—it was a matter of everybody getting along and trying to do one thing, and that's win."

Dooley knows full well how talented Kelly was, despite nitpicking by some critics. He called Kelly a truly great quarterback and said: "He could throw it. He was *strong*—he was a big guy, that's what impressed me about him. Kelly also had great competitiveness and leadership qualities." Tom Matte agreed, calling Kelly a "guy who would fight you in the trenches."

When Raymond Berry coached the New England Patriots, he went up against Kelly. "He and John Unitas have a whole lot in common. This guy is a tough, tough competitor. You can't intimidate Jim Kelly, that's for darn sure. He could throw the football and he could throw it really well. He could get it there. I mean, he was up there as good as you get. They both had great leadership ability, great competitiveness. Players just loved the guy, like they did John, and he also had a good coach and a good organization which gave him good players around him."

Berry noted that the two similar quarterbacks, Unitas and Kelly, "were affected by [their Pittsburgh] environment." He said it was much like the kids who grew up "in Texas in the years I was growing up. It was a state not very far removed from the frontier. They were one of the late ones coming in the union, and Texans are independent, hard-headed, and tough. That is true of Western Pennsylvania—there's too many guys of the same caliber [for it not to be true]. They come out of a tough background."

Former World Football League coach Andy Nelson chipped in, "He had his day there with Buffalo. He was a big, strong guy who could throw the ball. He was a tough fellow." Like Unitas, Kelly was respected for such a high degree of toughness. He may not have stuck mud up his nose to stem the flow of blood, but he took his lumps.

Ditka said, "Don't forget, Buffalo wasn't a very good football team until he got there. He was an outstanding quarterback. I don't think that they'll ever give him all the credit he deserves . . . but he was outstanding. To me, Jim was more of a team player than a lot of these guys."

Another quality that separates Kelly from some other great athletes is his total devotion to his family. A tender side of Kelly came out when he gave his acceptance speech the day he was enshrined in the Pro Football Hall of Fame. He spoke at some length of his son, Hunter, fittingly born on Valentine's Day (in 1997), also Jim's birthday. Hunter, Kelly said, was "the son I've always wanted. . . . But within four months, my son was diagnosed with a fatal nervous system disorder known as Krabbe's disease. They told us to take him home and make him comfortable. And from that day, my wife and I decided to fight this disease." He vowed to try his best to "make sure that kids all over the world don't suffer like my son does."

Kelly said he prayed his son would be with him when he was inducted into the Hall, adding "God has granted me that blessing.

"It has been written throughout my career that toughness is my trademark. Well, the toughest person I've ever met in my life is my hero, my soldier, my son, Hunter. I love you buddy." Sadly, three years later Hunter succumbed to the fatal nervous system disease, leaving his family at the age of eight.

SOFT COAL AND HARD QUARTERBACKS

Prevailing Theories for Western Pennsylvania's Quarterback Dominance

GIVEN THE ACCOMPLISHMENTS of The Six, it is irrefutable that Western Pennsylvania gave birth to way, way beyond its share of great quarterbacks. The questions remain: why and how? The truth is nobody knows for sure, but everyone seems to have a theory or two.

The area around Pittsburgh is famous for, among other things, soft coal and hard quarterbacks. Rick Volk, a teammate of Unitas, called him "just a hard-nosed guy—and I think that's the way everybody was back in those days from Western Pennsylvania, what with the coal mines and steel mills." Actually, of course, this issue is much more complex than that.

SPORTS AS A PRIORITY

Jeff Petrucci, who was Joe Montana's quarterback coach in high school, believes that athletics in the area always has been a priority. "When I was a kid, it was important to compete and to play. Your success came because of the success of your team."

Johnny Unitas's cousin Joe agreed. "Everybody who lived here in Western Pennsylvania—in the back streets, in the alleys—they always played football." Ex–NFL quarterback Scott Zolak stated: "At seven years old, it started with me being around my dad, around coaches, and it's just go-out-and-you-play, that's what you do in town. It's a competitive nature. It's Pittsburgh people. That's how we're raised. We didn't go to malls or hang out, we played sports around the clock."

Speer Ruey, a Western Pennsylvania athlete, said that his peers who loved football had one big goal in mind. "Everybody who could throw the ball wanted to be a quarterback."

POVERTY

Being poor motivated many athletes. All-American Arnold Galiffa, who is enshrined in the College Football Hall of Fame, used to practice football daily with his friends in an alley under Donora streetlights. Galiffa's friend and former Steeler Rudy Andabaker said, "We tore up cardboard boxes and used them for shoulder pads." Galiffa attended school while also working eight-hour shifts in the Donora mills, but he had dreams, and he never carped about his plight.

While the focus is on quarterbacks, many others also serve as examples of men who found better lives through football. Tony Dorsett, who was born in Rochester, Pennsylvania (as was quarterback Babe Parilli), attended Hopewell High School. He is the only man ever to win a championship in both college and pro football, capture a Heisman Trophy, and gain Hall of Fame status as both a collegian and a professional.

Dorsett's father worked hard in a steel mill to provide for his family. "My dad used to tell me, he said, 'Tony, you go into the steel mill, you're not guaranteed you're going to come out of the steel mill. . . . Every day I go into this place, I have to kiss my wife goodbye because I don't know if I'm coming back.'" His father prodded him, Tony said, to "get your education, make something of yourself. And that really stuck with me."

With the backing of a strong family, Dorsett soon saw his athletic ability lift his family out of poverty. At the University of Pittsburgh, Dorsett led the nation in rushing with 2,150 yards in his Heisman season as a senior, averaging nearly 180 rushing per game. His career yards-rushing total of 6,526 set an NCAA record, as did his 22 touchdowns in his senior year. He took a program that had posted a humiliating 1–11 record the year before he hit campus to a national championship in his fourth season.

Dorsett didn't slow down as a pro, either. In 1983, against Minnesota, he bolted for a record 99-yard run. He ran for 1,000 or more yards in each of his first nine NFL seasons, with the exception of a strike-shortened season in 1987. Not too shabby for a kid from the projects.

Just as necessity is the mother of invention, the success of athletes from Pittsburgh blue-collar families supports the theory that poverty often gives birth to ambition. Hunger pangs, both the literal and figurative varieties, are strong driving forces.

Donora's Ulice Payne, who was a member of Marquette University's national championship basketball team and later became the president of the Milwaukee Brewers, feels that poverty can still motivate, even though young players finding ample work in steel mills is now rare. Rare because so many mills vanished, like the pollution that lurked in the smoke that once rose from them like a mushroom cloud. Payne commented, "There's a different poverty there, but I still think there's a motivation for everybody to improve. Even though today the mill is gone, you can't forget them—there were guys who told you about the mill. It was within arm's reach to remind you that this is not what you wanted."

Many area youngsters witnessed the demolition of rusty smokestacks and other parts of the once productive steel mills as symbols of decline. Squinting intently for a bright side, such decay around them spurred them to work hard at sports, to seek a better future.

IMMIGRANTS AND WORK ETHIC

The immigrants who streamed into Western Pennsylvania—primarily from countries such as Germany, Italy, Poland, Russia, and Czechoslovakia—may have brought poverty with them, but they also brought along intangibles such as a strong gene pool, hope, ambition, drive, and determination.

Sportswriter Jim O'Brien stated that Western Pennsylvania settlers with Eastern European, Italian, and African American roots "turned out steel, zinc, and world-class athletes." Without a doubt, the area benefited from the rich genetic pool of talent that resided there.

Steel towns were magnets for hardworking immigrants, men who never shirked backbreaking, dirty work, hungry men who toiled diligently, glad to have the opportunity to work in America.

Consider, for instance, the pathetic plight of many Polish immigrants. In America most of them took jobs in mines, steel mills, and slaughterhouses, seeking jobs where they could quickly make money. More often than not, that required them to accept mindless, perilous work.

One Polish immigrant commented: "I came to America because I heard the streets were paved with gold. When I got here I found out three things: First, the streets weren't paved with gold. Second, they weren't paved at all. Third, I was expected to pave them."

The sons of such hardy men witnessed their fathers trudge to work then return, soiled and weary, but unbroken, and they quickly learned what a strong work ethic meant. As athletes, they were, to paraphrase

Carl Sandburg's definition of *slang*, the kind of men who rolled up their sleeves, spat on their hands, and got to work.

Many great athletes were raised by immigrant fathers who possessed a shot-and-a-beer, "ask no quarter, give no quarter" mentality. They may not have always given children a wholesome *Leave It to Beaver* middle-class childhood, but they surely did generate young players who were as tough as the nails produced in a steel mill wireworks. Tom Callahan's book, *Johnny U.,* contains a Babe Parilli quotation that sums up the spirit of Western Pennsylvanians: "The kids got out of the mills and the mines, but they stayed mills and mines kids."

Mike Ditka, who epitomized the term "smash-mouth football" long before the phrase was coined, noted: "It's contrary to what America does today—we don't encourage people to work. But it was a badge of courage and a badge of pride for these people to go to work eight hours every day, to earn a paycheck, to come home to feed their families and put their kids in school. That was important. There was a lot of pride involved in those people. They had a value system that was special, it worked. It was what America was built on."

Many African Americans also populated the Pittsburgh area. One, John Woodruff, won a gold medal in the 1936 Olympics as a member of the U.S. track and field team. That unit featured 10 African Americans, who scored enough points to have won the track and field championship by themselves.

It wasn't until more recent times that African Americans became quarterbacks with any degree of regularity; there are logical, but unfair reasons for that. For one thing, at first football shunned Africa American athletes—as late as 1951, there were only 14 African Americans in the NFL. One prejudiced view espoused by white owners and coaches was that African Americans weren't smart enough to be quarterbacks. Believing that, they simply didn't let those men play there.

Unitas, of Lithuanian roots, felt that Western Pennsylvania stars from Lujack through Montana had a common trait, their "no-nonsense, blue-collar background." Unitas's son Chad said his father was a "hard-working guy from a blue-collar, hard-working town."

Surprisingly, the toughness of The Six did not ensure them superstar status in collegiate football—none won the Heisman Trophy; remark-ably, the highest finish in Heisman voting for a member of The Six was the fourth-place showing by Dan Marino. Another stunning fact that illustrates the same point: To date, only Marino has been inducted into the College Football Hall of Fame.

Montana, unable to solve the Western Pennsylvania quarterback enigma, often resorts to the facetious "it's in the water" explanation. However, he also threw in the name of a Pittsburgh beer, saying, "It might have been something in the water. Maybe it was in the Iron City beer."

Baseball writer and analyst Bill James, well aware of the glowing and astonishing reputation of Donora, Pennsylvania, when it comes to producing great athletes, summed up what he perceived to be an Achilles-like phenomenon, "My son is a ballplayer; I'm thinking of taking him to be washed in the waters of Donora." Those very same waters, of the Monongahela River, also were used to bathe other greats such as the Griffeys and Montana.

Detroit Lions linebacker Mike Lucci, also from Western Pennsylvania, dismissed all flippant talk of the powers of water:

> When you did something, you were expected to do it to your fullest ability, and I think the work ethic has a lot to do about it. When you think about Namath and Kelly or Marino and Montana, I don't think there was something in the water, and they said, "Okay we're going to be good quarterbacks," but I think there was something there that made them good, and an intangible desire to succeed.
>
> When I was growing up, you were expected to carry your end of the load. The expectations were that you would bust your ass to be a part of the team and to excel. I think a little bit of it is that Western Pennsylvania work ethic.

FAMILY INFLUENCE

Jeff Petrucci said, "I think the attitude of Western Pennsylvania people basically [stemmed from them coming] from two-parent homes. They had direction, they had discipline, they had love, and those were all very important things for the success of an individual. Obviously a lot of kids come from single-parent homes, and they're very successful—I don't mean this in a negative way. But I think back to [The Six], and as far as I'm aware, they all came from two-parent homes." Almost all—Joe Namath is one exception.

"Marino grew up with a mother and a dad. He was like Montana. If Joe was playing in hell, mom and dad would have been on the 40-yard line, that's the way it was. It was that kind of relationship—they were very, very close and very caring and loving to one another."

Marino's family lived an unassuming life in a cozy home in the Oakland section of Pittsburgh. Stability was a part of his upbringing. For example, his father lived in the same neighborhood for nearly 60 years. In Marino's Hall of Fame acceptance speech, he called his dad his hero, role model, and the best coach he ever encountered. "You taught me how to throw a football, you taught me about hard work and how to be positive. I'll always remember the times that we'd just sit and talk about football and about life. . . . You would always say that you didn't deserve anything in life; you only deserve what you earn."

Unitas's background was humble. His father, who passed away when John was very young, earned a living delivering coal. Chad Unitas said, "His mother had to work two jobs to put food on the table and clothes on his and his siblings' backs." John's mother, to use a sports phrase, led by example. Chad said, "She was wonderful—she instilled in him that if he wanted to get something done, then he had needed to put the work and time into it." Unitas once said he learned more lessons from his mother than from any of his coaches "about being tough, about hanging in there. She was a tough, tough lady."

In the instance of another Western Pennsylvania athlete, it was a brother who provided the support a young quarterback needed. When Italian American Arnold Galiffa complained of the hazing he had to endure as a West Point plebe, his older brother Frank told him he wouldn't allow him to transfer to another school. "Not many people of our nationality get to go to Army," he informed Arnold. "It's an honor. So you're staying. I'll kick your ass if you think about leaving Army."

Among The Six, only the rebellious Namath came from a broken home. Still, Namath did have a father figure in his high school coach Larry Bruno, who treated him benevolently.

Meanwhile, Paul Zolak gave Joe Montana Sr. a lot of credit. "He played a major role in his son's development. He would drive Joe, an only child, everywhere. And in the summer, after a baseball game, everybody would leave and Joe would take off his uniform. He and his dad would go out into centerfield and work on three-step and seven-step drop patterns, and he would be the center for Joe."

Mark Gorscak, a high school teammate of Montana, said, "Joe's motivation was his father, who was always around at all the practices. I think he got pushed by his father, just because he was always around."

Ulice Payne recalled Joe Sr. coaching his son in various sports. "He and his father had an interesting relationship. Maybe his father saw himself in him, but he would be on Joe's ass, but it didn't seem to bother him. He was hard on Joe, but it was love." Payne said at times Joe would execute a difficult play that his father had specifically told him not to try, perhaps as a personal challenge to him, prompting an attitude of "somehow, I *can* do it," which must have carried over to his many comebacks.

There are times when a father's influence is transmitted by osmosis, rather than intention. Paul Zolak said that his son Scott, a former NFL quarterback, gained one big edge by chance: "Because I was coaching when he was in high school, he was always around football. When Joey [Montana] was 17, Scott was 7, so he was always on the Ringgold High School sidelines. Joey would kick off, and Scott would run out and get the tee. That exposure [is important]. I know Bill Parcells talks about this—a lot of the great quarterbacks, he calls them gym rats, had fathers who were coaches, and they're exposed to the elements of football all the time." Scott Zolak claims this exposure helped him in his professional development: "It's how football was born in my blood."

COMMUNITY AND ROLE MODELS

Then there's the concept of young athletes striving to follow in the "cleatprints" of Western Pennsylvania predecessors who were football stars. "Jumbo" Jim Covert of Conway, Pennsylvania, was voted to the Pro Football Hall of Fame's First Team All-1980s. He once said, "Football is almost like a religion. . . . And, you know, you see the great players that come from this area, and go on to bigger and better things, and I wanted that for myself."

David Sarkus, who was Montana's backup in high school, stated, "Culture is passed on, through storytelling, through photographs, video today." Sports, he stated, became the motivation to gain recognition for "physical excellence. It is a deeply ingrained part of this culture. Joe came from very humble beginnings, and I think what inspired him was seeing the athletes around him and hearing the stories of great athletes who had gone before him. I think Joe was caught up in that culture of excellence in sports. As most any person realizes when they're growing up, there are certain things they find that they do well and get praised and applauded for. Athletics were essential to our culture and community. So when you excel in sports, you're elevated to another level."

Dick Bestwick was a college coach and a national scout for the Dallas Cowboys. He observed: "Once you get one [player to achieve], you have all these others trying to emulate him. There have always been guys to look up to in Western Pennsylvania—you had role models that you aspired to be as good as. They serve as an inspiration to other kids."

So nearly all young boys growing up around Pittsburgh played football, pretending to be, say, a Johnny Unitas; a select handful would go on to make it big. Beaver Falls native Steve Higgins is the director of a foundation there named after Namath's high school coach. He said Namath looked up to local quarterbacks, having heroes like Babe Parilli "from Rochester, right down the road from Beaver Falls, and Lou D'Achille, who was called the left-handed Lujack."

Dan Towler came from Donora and said that young athletes growing up in town looked at the greats who had preceded them as "a point of pride to the community. Athletics was what made the community a community. . . . Quite often, the way the town celebrated was through its teams."

Tom Caudill said of many Western Pennsylvania towns: "These were bedrock communities. The parents were involved with the kids. Athletic prowess and success meant an awful lot—they took a lot of pride in Friday night games." It seems only natural, then, that if a town earns a strong reputation for manufacturing great athletes, young residents will leap on the athletic bandwagon. Many of them will ultimately perpetuate the town's athletic success.

Once involved in something they love, youngsters often routinely continue down that road, almost as if their next step is preordained. Don Yannessa was a successful coach for Ambridge, Aliquippa, and Baldwin high schools. Ambridge sent eight of their natives to the NFL, including star linebacker Mike Lucci. Yannessa pointed out, "Being on the high school team was a big deal when I was growing up. Everybody I knew played on the football team and went to college."

Aliquippa's football program has been so rich in tradition that aspiring football players are naturally lured to go out for the sport. As early as the 1980s, Yannessa had fireworks displays featured at the Quips' home games. One long-standing pregame tradition features an Indian mascot, named Chief Aliquippa, gallop onto the field, make his way to midfield and plunge a flaming spear into the ground. Petrucci observed, "It's the 'takes a community to raise a child' saying. That's one of the big reasons there was success in Western Pennsylvania in those times."

Namath once reflected upon his family and friends. "If it wasn't for these people . . . old Joe might have been some place else altogether. There'll always be Beaver Falls and Joe Namath."

Paul Zolak spoke of how his son Scott followed Montana's footsteps. "At a party Joe gave Scott a football, and he had written on it, 'Scott, good luck in your senior year. See you in the NFL one day.' You get goose bumps just thinking about it."

Scott said that gesture "was pretty important" to him, and he did enjoy a good senior year. In his second year with the New England Patriots, Scott got his first NFL start. "Scott was very superstitious when he was at the University of Maryland," began his father, "and he always rubbed the [Montana-signed] football before a game. The ball was back at home, and Scott found out a few days before the game that he was going to start." The ball was shipped overnight, and Scott got it on game day. "He rubs the football and, lo and behold, he has a great game, and New England won their first game of the year, and he got the Offensive MVP that week in the NFL. It was all about the ball," concluded Zolak with a chuckle.

Perhaps it truly wasn't all about the ball, but it was a case of an older player from the same community inspiring a younger quarterback. Such a bond is emblematic of the strong sense of community in Western Pennsylvania.

SELF-CONFIDENCE AND SELF-FULFILLING PROPHECIES

There's a psychological concept known as the self-fulfilling prophecy, and it often applies to sports. Simply stated, if a person goes into a venture, even one as simple as shooting a foul shot, and he believes he will or will not make the shot, he will live out that belief, that prophecy, by either calmly making the shot or by choking. He may even say, "See? I just knew I would/wouldn't miss that shot."

One study indicates players who believe they will fail tend to internalize, questioning their actions, "Am I releasing the ball properly?" The greats—more focused, with little if any self-doubt—are impervious to such self-exploration. For them it's a matter of trusting one's self—"Just let the ball fly." Money players such as Montana seemingly will themselves to win. As they come to believe in themselves, they find success over and over again.

In clutch moments, exuding an aura of self-confidence and great leadership, such men bark out words such as, "After we complete this sideline pass, I'm going to hit Jerry Rice on a post pattern to win it." The word *after* is used, assuming success; he didn't say, "*If* we complete the sideline pass." Positive phrasing stamps an imprimatur, a guarantee of success.

Mark Gorscak remembered Montana, his high school teammate, as "a quiet kid—he spoke when he needed to, and he was always calm." Confident, he would remained unruffled, even under the dire duress of, say, a heavy NFL blitz—the kind in which a quarterback can feel and smell the rancid exhale of a fire-breathing linebacker as he prepares to pounce. Ken Thomas, who went to high school with Namath, said, "He had that cockiness, a hot dog attitude, or maybe it was more self-assuredness, but I think it was a part of that attitude that makes athletes great—a self-confidence."

For a quarterback to succeed, he also must cope with pressure. Professors Bruce Ogilvie and Thomas Tutko studied myriad athletes and concluded in their book *The Psychology of Baseball* that athletes "often must face in hours or days the kind of pressure that occurs in the life of the achievement-oriented man over several years." They also concluded that the greats, such as The Six, share traits such as outstanding leadership, determination, the willingness to make sacrifices, conscientiousness, and the ability to peak under pressure. Such men *will* act out positive self-fulfilling prophecies over and over again.

Marino said, "If you ask any great player or quarterback, there's a certain inner confidence that you're as good as anybody." Unitas concurred, "There is a difference between conceit and confidence. Conceit is bragging about yourself. Confidence means you believe you can get the job done." Namath was cocky, bordering on arrogant when it came to his self-image. Larry Bruno noted, "There's a difference between being cocky and confident. . . . A quarterback has to be [confident]; the team has to feed on that."

Bruno told of a time when his Beaver Falls team faced Aliquippa and had a fourth-and-long situation late in the game. Fearing his quarterback, who also did the team's punting, was drained, Bruno asked Namath if he was going to have enough steam to get off a good punt. "He put his arm around me," began Bruno, "and looked me right in the eye and he said, 'Coach, we're not going to have to punt.'" He was right, and his team went on to win.

Then there was the time Namath unequivocally stated the Colts would fall to the Jets in Super Bowl III. Teammate Dave Herman said, "Joe believed it. He really thought we were going to beat them. And eventually, we all did."

COMPETITIVE NATURE

While it's true that all great athletes are very competitive, somehow Western Pennsylvania stars have—or believe they have—an overabundance of this attribute. Ditka, who serves as the personification of a bulldog of a player, said that *everything* in his life was competitive. "My whole life was based on beating the other guy, being equal to, showing that I could be as good as anybody else. That's the way I grew up."

Ditka was as tough and hard as anthracite coal. Even when he was a rookie, he matter-of-factly said he refused "to take any guff." He added that he heard veterans saying, "Let's knock his can off," but his response was a succinct "I don't think they can." One college coach told *Sport* magazine, "That kid is the only guy I know who could make it through Dante's Inferno."

Ditka, who entered Pitt with the intention of becoming a dentist, dished out "thundering blocks and stiff arms . . . knocking out the very teeth he had hoped to one day examine." He also became the first tight end ever inducted into the Pro Football Hall of Fame.

An expert on toughness, he marveled at The Six:

Joe Namath was tough, man. I love Joe Namath and Joe Montana. You say tough? There's a lot of different [types]—physical toughness, mental toughness. The mental toughness is what people don't see all the time, and that's what's really important. They were tough physically. I mean, they weren't imposing physically, but they were tough. Namath played his career on a leg that nobody else would have played on.

Montana was unbelievable. All you had to do was coach against him if you want to know how good he was. And Danny's special to me because he came out of Pittsburgh, he went to Pitt, and we kinda had the same background.

When Johnny Lujack was "an unheralded freshman" at Notre Dame, he was initially "lumped with the rest of the cannon fodder, the rinkydinks, the shit squad. These were the names for freshmen and other scrubs, who got pulverized by the varsity daily at practice," wrote Steve Delsohn in his book, *Talking Irish*. However, continued Delsohn, Lujack, in true Western Pennsylvania fashion, "distinguished himself quickly, running and tackling so hard [head coach Frank] Leahy knew his name the first week of practice."

A year later, when Angelo Bertelli left the Notre Dame campus and hopped a train headed for Paris Island to become a Marine, Lujack took over as the quarterback. His teammates' reaction at first proved they had yet to fathom Lujack's competitive ways and skill. Ed Mieszkowski said, "Lujack was *eighteen* his sophomore year. . . . So sure we had reservations about Lujack. You're going from Bertelli to a kid who's barely played. It's like trading in a Cadillac for a Volkswagen. The rest is history, right? Lujack passed for two touchdowns. He ran for another TD. We destroyed a good Army team, 26–0." He guided the Irish to a 9–1 record and the national championship.

Incidentally, after that season, it was Lujack's turn to depart South Bend and head out to serve his country. When he returned after a hiatus of close to three years for the 1946 and 1947 seasons, he was back at quarterback with no apparent rustiness. He then led a team that *Sports Illustrated* praised to the hilt: "Notre Dame fielded the greatest college football team in history, but which unbeaten Irish juggernaut was it: the 1946 or 1947 squad?" In Lujack's three seasons, the Fighting Irish put up a sensational record of 26–1–1 and won three national titles. Delsohn wrote that many fans insist "Lujack still remains the finest quarterback in Notre Dame history." Clearly, the competitive nature of Lujack, who won the 1947 Heisman Trophy, was a key.

Frank Tripucka, another Notre Dame quarterback (1945–48), called Lujack "probably the greatest all-around athlete I've ever seen in college football." In Steve Delsohn's *Talking Irish*, Tripucka pointed out that Lujack weighed only around 180 pounds, "but he was just a very tough guy from Western Pennsylvania. It probably showed the most when Lujack played on defense. He'd come up and hit people head-on." Writer Dan Jenkins selected Lujack as his second-best college quarterback ever, while another highly respected writer, Blackie Sherrod, listed Lujack as the best defensive back he ever saw on a college gridiron.

Meanwhile, Montana spoke proudly of the impact of his background. "It's just the nature of Western Pennsylvania. It really put a sense of value to what you're doing in sports. As far as I know, that's where I got my competitiveness from. Everything we did was competitive—whether it was pickup basketball, pickup football—it was you're playing the game to win."

Paul Zolak said, "That was Joe [Montana]—he had to win in everything, whether it was ping-pong or whatever. The biggest thing was his desire to win. He had that edge. And no matter what he was doing, he was going to do it 100 percent. You hate to lose, and sometimes the drive is more the hate to lose more so than the will to win."

Ulice Payne played high school basketball with Montana and shed light on the greatness of Western Pennsylvania athletes. "I just attribute it to high school football being based upon the industrial complex in Western Pennsylvania—each town was a part of the steel mill process, very competitive, yet connected, and I think that created an environment of competition at a very high level. And the quarterback position is the leader."

Perhaps the never-say-die competitive nature of Western Pennsylvania's great quarterbacks can be summarized, or at least illuminated, with one statistic: fourth-quarter comebacks, a stat kept since 1960. According to pro-football-reference.com, only Peyton Manning (with 45 such dramatic drives) and Tom Brady (39) rank above Marino (36) and Unitas (36), who are tied at No. 3. Montana is No. 6 on the list (31), Kelly stands No. 20 (22), and Blanda is No. 47 (17). Of The Six, only Namath falls out of the top 50—just barely, at No. 57 (16).

GOOD COACHING

Other states can lay claim to having great coaches, too, but the fact that the Pittsburgh area had more than its share of standout coaches is a factor as to why the region has churned out a multitude of football stars. Start with Dan Yannessa, who won four "AAA" championships at Aliquippa over a 17-season stretch. As a matter of fact, when the author of *Friday Night Lights* was seeking a high school as the focus for his book, he considered using Aliquippa.

The list of top-10 Western Pennsylvania high school football coaches (as ranked by Pittsburgh's *Tribune-Review* in 2006) placed Chuck Klausing (Braddock and Pitcairn) as No. 1, followed by Lindy Lauro (New Castle), Jim Render (Upper St. Clair), Pete Antimarino (Gateway), Jack McCurry (North Hills), Art Bernardi (Butler), Larry Bruno (Monaca and Beaver

Falls), Art Walker Sr. (Mt. Lebanon and Shady Side Academy), George Novak (Steel Valley and Woodland Hills), and Yannessa (Aliquippa).

Richard Mongelluzzo, a longtime high school football coach at Donora and Bethel Park, said he'd stack such men up against any area's coaches. "Absolutely. Take a look at the quarterbacks who came from Western Pennsylvania. It's amazing how many great ones came from this little niche." He argues that mediocre coaches could not turn out *so many* greats, kids that shone as early on as youth football and high school. The coaches frequently helped nurture latent talent or took talent that was already in evidence and raised it to another level.

Amateur-level football official Pete Carbonaro said another factor was the coaches' style of play for many schools. "When guys like Montana were in high school, they ran the pro set, which prepared them for later success. You got to have the footwork and the arm, but it didn't hurt to grow up playing out of the pro set."

Paul Zolak agreed. "I think those little things are the important. There are a lot of people now running the spread offense or the veer or the option offense. It's not the straight drop-back of Joe Montana or Dan Marino."

Clearly, many factors were in play to make Western Pennsylvania an incubator for budding, great football players. The bottom line is clear—to attribute the stellar careers of players such as The Six and other Hall of Famers such as Ditka to one cause is far too simplistic.

EPILOGUE
Final Thoughts

PERHAPS THE QUESTION of why Western Pennsylvania has produced so many great quarterbacks is not the proper question. Some experts take a broader view, saying Western Pennsylvania manufactures *great athletes.* Period.

Start with one small town, Donora, which nestles on the Monongahela River, a few miles from Montana's hometown, and just an hour's drive south of Pittsburgh. This self-proclaimed "Home of Champions" can serve as a microcosm for all of Western Pennsylvania.

In 1948, an insidious smog, caused by unusual weather conditions coupled with the pollution that the town's United States Steel mill spewed out of its smokestacks, engulfed Donorans in lethal fumes.

Even though death and severe illness knocked on Donora's door, the resilient town hosted their high school football game against Monongahela. Visibility was so poor that fans reportedly lost sight of punts when they sailed into afternoon skies. One writer called the contest, "the greatest game *never* seen." Rebounding from the suffocating tragedy, the town continued to prolifically turn out great athletes.

Donora's Ulice Payne was a member of Marquette's 1977 NCAA basketball championship team. When asked to explain his success, he replied, "I was born in the Home of Champions. That's what we do back there, win."

The *Saturday Evening Post* ran an article in October 1955 entitled "The Town That Spawns Athletes," touting Donora's crop of football players, which "always flourishes," focusing on Arnold "Pope" Galiffa, "Deacon" Dan Towler, and Stan Musial—a Pope, a deacon, and a Cardinal.

A half century later, they could have added the names of two other baseball standouts in Ken Griffey Sr. and his future Hall of Fame offspring, "Junior." The town also was home to Steve Filipowicz who was the sixth player taken in the 1943 NFL draft, who also played three seasons of major league baseball.

The town's greatest sports product, despite the excellence of Griffey Jr. was, of course, Stan "The Man." He and "Junior" happen to share the same birthdate. When they first met, Musial, borrowing a line from a sportswriter, teased the young Griffey, telling him that he was "the second-best left-handed hitting, left-handed throwing outfielder ever born in Donora, Pennsylvania, on November 21."

Many of the town's young athletes started their road to a better life by attending college, and many of them did so thanks to their football prowess. The *Saturday Evening Post* article on Donora athletes noted, "In recent years 211 boys from Donora have received athletic scholarships at U.S. colleges." The town mass-produced stars much as its U.S. Steel mill shipped out zinc, wire, and steel products. In the fall of 1955 alone, "more than two dozen Donora boys" were expected to see action in college contests.

Through the 1954 season, the high school's legendary football coach, Jim Russell, had led his Dragons to a 134–35 record and had won the Western Pennsylvania Interscholastic Athletic League (WPIAL) championship in 9 of the previous 14 seasons. His squad even knocked off (by a lopsided 35–7 score) a New Kensingston team that sent six of its starters to Michigan State, players who later helped the Spartans make it to a Rose Bowl game. In the 1942 and 1943 scholastic play-offs, Donora faced Turtle Creek, a team that featured a future Notre Dame All-American in Leon Hart, who later became the last lineman to win the Heisman Trophy (1949), and the Dragons crushed them twice.

Russell gathered his players at their home facility, Legion Field, and made it a point to inform his troops: "There are two roads from this field. One leads down that hill to the mill. If you want to be just another fellow making some sort of living, then don't bother to work hard out here. The mill is where you'll wind up. But if you really want to make something out of yourself, play football hard and study hard. Then you can take the road out of here to a good college."

One such player was Arnold Galiffa, an All-State quarterback who led the team that is considered to be the best high school team in Western Pennsylvania history, the 1945 Dragons. At West Point he was an All-American quarterback who won 11 total varsity letters, second most in school history—in football (back when freshmen were not permitted to play on the varsity squad), baseball, and basketball. In 1949, he finished fourth in the voting for the Heisman Trophy. Galiffa made it to the NFL and to the Canadian Football League before injuries curtailed his career.

Louis "Bimbo" Cecconi took over Galiffa's Donora quarterback duties. Cecconi said that when Galiffa served in the Korean War, armed with a hand grenade instead of a football, he launched a grenade into a sniper's nest. "They said in a book that he threw it 75 yards. It's hard to figure somebody throwing it that far, but I say, 'I don't care if it was 40, 50, 60, or 70: he threw it, and he was in the battle, and that's what counts.'"

Cecconi himself took the Donora torch from Galiffa, later becoming a four-year starter (1946–49) for Pitt as their quarterback and halfback. Twice he led Pitt in all-purpose yards and stood third in school history for total offense (3,781 yards). At one time, he also held the team record for the longest touchdown pass, an 82-yard strike in 1948 to yet another Donora native, Nick DeRosa.

Meanwhile, Dan Towler made All-State in 1944 and 1945, helping his Dragons go undefeated while notching back-to-back WPIAL football titles. In fact, the 1945 Dragon defense never relinquished a score. The only time an opponent crossed the Donora goal line was on a fumble recovery. The team was ranked by a major sports publication as the second best high school team in the nation, behind only a Texas team that featured football legends Bobby Layne and Doak Walker. At Washington and Jefferson, Towler made the Associated Press Little All-American team three times and set a school record, which still stands, when he averaged 16.6 points scored over his eight games in his junior gridiron season.

Towler was a bruising fullback for the Los Angeles Rams in the era of Bob Waterfield, Norm Van Brocklin, and Elroy "Crazy Legs" Hirsch. Called "one of the greatest runners there was" by NFL chief scout Red Hickey, Towler led the NFL with his 894 rushing yards in 1952. That year the four-time All-Pro was good for 75 yards per game on the ground for a whopping average of 5.7 yards per carry—very impressive, but down from his 6.8 yards per rush in 1951, which then represented the sixth best average in NFL history for a single season. In addition, through the 2012 season that average still placed him in the top 15 all-time, topping the best mark ever achieved by men such as Jim Brown (6.4) and Gale Sayers (6.2). His average yards rushing per game over his career ranked No. 10 all-time when he retired, and he owned a hefty average of 5.2 yards every time he toted the ball. Plus his total yards rushing stood as a team record for two decades. Many years later the all-time Rams team was selected with two running backs chosen, Eric Dickerson and Towler.

Back in 1955, the average graduating class of Donora High was roughly 125 students. Of that co-ed population, around 17 boys usually received athletic scholarships. At that time, Boston University's football coach Buff Donelli said: "You can always tell a Donora guy. I've coached them. No matter how many letters he has won, he still runs like a rookie. He's afraid the town will catch up with him." And a Notre Dame football coach of that era, Terry Brennan, appraised Donora's Bob Gaydos, a guard, saying: "He seems to have that extra something peculiar to all Donora athletes. He has terrific spirit and more determination to be a Notre Dame football player than anybody you'd want to see. He never lets up."

College coaches quickly sought out more and more Donora players. The town became, in effect, a brand name that could be trusted.

Dale Stewart, who played his high school ball for Donora, was a fullback for Carnegie Institute of Technology (now Carnegie Mellon University). Rugged and strong, he was the same type of running back as Leroy Heard, the man who reportedly said, "Coach, if you need one yard, I'll get you three. If you need five yards, I'll get you three."

Stewart called himself "a lead back who loved to block, and a short yardage back. I scored about six or seven touchdowns, but the sum total of all the touchdowns was probably 13 yards." His college coach once told him, half-admiringly, half-candidly, "Stewart, you're a hard-nosed Western Pennsylvania boy, but you're probably the slowest back I've ever coached." Perhaps, but the hard-nosed Stewart plugged away game after game.

After the graduation of Donora's class of 1969—a group that included Griffey Sr., a star player in four sports—students from Donora and Monongahela high schools were combined to form Ringgold High School, which produced Joe Montana. If one tosses Monongahela and Ringgold schools into the Donora equation for the purposes of this chapter, the list of football talent becomes so thick in that vicinity that one website, pittsburghquarterback.com, ranked the Donora-Monongahela-Ringgold schools as the greatest district (from 1946 on) for manufacturing boys who went on to play the quarterback position for a Division I college or for a pro team, including not only the NFL, but also the Canadian Football League and the Arena Football League (see appendix 1).

In the ranking, each player was given a point value based on the quality of his career. One point was the point value awarded to men who started at a major college for at least the bulk of one season. A two-point rating indicated that the player was a significant college quarterback, a "team leader," on a national stage. If a player made it to the NFL, he earned an evaluation of three points; if a player was a prominent NFL quarterback, he received four points. A player such as Montana scored the highest grade of all, 4.5 points, for attaining Hall of Fame status.

In addition to Montana, there were four other players from the Donora/Monongahela area who were evaluated. Cecconi scored 2.0 points for being the University of Pittsburgh's leading passer in 1948 and 1949. He also was drafted by the 49ers. Next was Arnold Galiffa, who scored a 3.0 for having been inducted into the College Football Hall of Fame and for having made it to the NFL.

Arnold's nephew Bernie Galiffa garnered a 1.5 evaluation as a starter for West Virginia University under Bobby Bowden. He had also been a second-team All-State quarterback and earned a spot in the prestigious "Faces in the Crowd" column in *Sports Illustrated*. The magazine noted that Bernie Galiffa clicked on 88 of 149 passes as a senior, good for 22 touchdowns and 1,890 yards in 9 games, "to surpass Joe Namath's Western Pennsylvania mark (77 of 125 for 1,115 [yards] and 17 [TDs])." Galiffa didn't merely break, he *shattered* Namath's records for yardage through the air and touchdowns. Overall, he completed 53 percent of his passes for 3,858 yards, often hitting the fleet Griffey Sr. on long heaves.

Galiffa was a starter at WVU in 1971 and 1972, the year WVU finished sixth in the nation for passing and fourth for scoring offense. He threw for 1,543 yards and 8 TDs as a junior. The next year, he threw 17 touchdowns and 2,496 yards (still in the top 10 in WVU history) to become the first quarterback in school history to throw for 2,000+ yards. He held the West Virginia University record for yards passing in a season and a career (4,426) until Marc Bulger, born in Pittsburgh, surpassed him. Galiffa said, "Now they're just blowing my records out of the water. Those guys throw the ball every down."

Scott Zolak was the fifth quarterback of significance who came from the Donora/Monongahela region. He earned a 3.0 mark on the pittsburghquarterback.com list for his days as a quarterback at the University of Maryland and for his eight-year career in the NFL. All of the quarterbacks on this list were from Donora with the exceptions of Ringgold graduates Zolak and Montana.

Remember, though, Donora doesn't exist in isolation—again, the town represents something that is shared by all of Western Pennsylvania. Numerous other small towns had prolific athletic outputs. For example, in addition to being the hometown of Johnny Lujack, who took Notre Dame to three national titles and won the Heisman Trophy, Connellsville also turned out John Woodruff, the grandson of a slave, who took home an Olympic gold medal for the 800-meter run in the 1936 games in Berlin, Germany, winning it in front of a fuming Adolf Hitler.

Connellsville, known for its coke foundries, was also the home of Wally Shroyer, who became a starter at running back as a freshman at Penn State University; major leaguers Gene Hasson and Bob Bailor; and Dick Pitzer, an All-American wide receiver at Army. In Pitzer and Lujack, Connellsville turned out young men who played on five straight national champions (from 1943 through 1947).

The area in and around Aliquippa produced many stars, including Mike Ditka; Tony Dorsett, who attended Hopewell High; Ty Law; Darrelle Revis; basketball legend "Pistol" Pete Maravich; baseball's Tito and Terry Francona (both from New Brighton High); Doc Medich; and Pete Suder.

Still, the question of why this area's most valuable export has been quarterbacks lingers. There are other places in the nation where similar conditions have existed, and those areas didn't churn out quarterbacks like Model-Ts rolling off early assembly lines.

Ulice Payne, reflecting on The Six, observed: "You can say it's all co-incidence, but that's a heckuva percentage for coincidence. It's not sci-entific. You can't figure it out, but it's happening. The phenomenon is there, right? There are other [hotbeds for athletes], but not like this, *not like this.*"

Many individual theories were touched upon earlier concerning how Western Pennsylvania defied all odds by turning out so many greats, but the truth may be this: There is no *single* theory to account for the over-abundance of tremendous athletes/quarterbacks who came out of the sports mecca known as Western Pennsylvania. Rather, like the conflu-ence of Pittsburgh's three rivers, many factors flowed together to create the phenomenon.

Vince Dooley has been an astute observer of the game for decades. His theory on Western Pennsylvania's talent pool is simple, but viable—an Occam's razor–like theory. He says such an anomaly can occur because, like any strange coincidence, inexplicable things simply *do occur,* albeit very rarely. He drew a parallel to baseball. "You can go down to Mo-bile, Alabama, and you'll find there are more Hall of Famers in baseball from that little bitty town [than seems normal]. It's just something that happens, you don't know how to explain it." Call it a fortuitous football anomaly. Perhaps it's like the magic Santa holds for children who can't fathom just how old Saint Nick can circumnavigate the globe each Christmas Eve to once again come through with their cornucopia of booty: It just happens.

Sadly the rich Western Pennsylvania output isn't what it had been. Marino, the last of The Six to retire, departed after the 1996 season. The population of many old Western Pennsylvania mill towns has dwindled, decreasing the total number of athletes coming from the area. The fictional town of Maycomb in *To Kill A Mockingbird* was called an old and tired town. By way of comparison, many steel towns have become enervated, almost decrepit locales. Some resemble ghost towns out of an old cowboy movie.

In the decade of the 1970s, a survey listed the top U.S. counties for producing major college football recruits. Allegheny County was the third highest rated county. Further, based upon per capita statistics, a staggering five of the most prolific counties in the entire nation were from southwestern Pennsylvania, with Beaver County coming in second. Westmorland, Washington, Fayette, and Allegheny counties ranked sixth, seventh, eighth, and eleventh.

Also, in 1979, well over 45,000 Pennsylvania students played high school football. A startling contrast was evident 20 years later—that figure plummeted to a 24,245, a precipitous drop of almost exactly 47 percent. Meanwhile, Texas saw a rise of more than 100 percent in their high school students' involvement in football, soaring from 77,037 to 159,535.

People from the Pittsburgh vicinity can, nevertheless, console themselves and maintain their pride in their sports legacy. After all, they are fully aware that what happened within their cradle of quarterbacks is even now unmatched.

Appendix 2 illustrates an obscure but impressive point about the Hall of Fame stranglehold of The Six. It focuses on four major quarterback categories: completions, percentage of passes completed, yards thrown, and touchdown passes. It reveals that every one of our Western Pennsylvania greats finished his career in the top 10 for at least one of those categories.

Joe Namath finished his playing days in the top 10 in one department; George Blanda and Jim Kelly cracked the top 10 in three of those realms; and Joe Montana, Dan Marino, and John Unitas all hung up their cleats among the top 10 in all four categories. In fact, Marino and Unitas ended their careers ranking No. 1, No. 1, No. 1, and No. 9, respectively, in the statistical departments. The top-10 measuring stick allows one to compare The Six with their contemporaries and with those who preceded them to show how they stacked up with the all-time greatest statistical outputs to that point.

The area around Pittsburgh that produced The Six covers about 7,854 square miles. The entire area of the United States is roughly 3,800,000. Therefore, the Pittsburgh vicinity discussed in this book accounts for far less than 1 percent (.002), or just one-fifth of a percent, of the total area of our country. For such a sliver of our nation to be responsible for so many great quarterbacks is unfathomable, prompting a "What are the odds?!" response.

Furthermore, as mentioned in chapter 1, The Six made up more than 25 percent of all the modern-era quarterbacks in the Pro Football Hall of Fame not too long ago. Even after Kurt Warner joined the Hall of Fame in 2017, 6 of the 27 modern-day quarterbacks enshrined there are the men who are the focal point of this book, still an astronomically high percentage. Actually, that fact alone sums it up: No other part of the country has ever had such a veritable monopoly, such a historic stranglehold, on football's most important position, and it's highly doubtful any area will ever match the sheer extravagance of Western Pennsylvania in producing quarterback talent.

1

PARTIAL LIST OF STAR WESTERN PENNSYLVANIA QUARTERBACKS FROM TOP AREA HIGH SCHOOLS

···
As Compiled by pittsburghquarterback.com

THIS LIST CONSIDERED quarterbacks from 1946 on who went on to become starting quarterbacks for a Division I college or played professional ball. Each player was graded for the quality of his career. Following is the point scale (although the evaluators gave half points in some instances):

- One point for being a starter at a major college for at least the bulk of one season
- Two points for being a significant college quarterback on a national stage
- Three points for being an NFL quarterback
- Four points for being a prominent NFL quarterback. However, in some cases a Hall of Famer such as Montana earned more than four points (4.5 for him).

The website also stated: "The rankings are primarily based upon geographical areas, rather than school district specific, since many schools have closed, or merged with other schools. For example, Ringgold came from Monongahela and Donora high schools. The ratings do not take into account the population of the area."

HONORABLE MENTIONS: MCKEESPORT AND UNIONTOWN

McKeesport: Ray Matthews, Ross Fichtner, Cecil Howard. Bill Brown played in the NFL, but was more of a running back and played last in the NFL in 1945
Uniontown: Fred Mazurek, Sandy Stephens, and Ed Chlebek

7TH: HOMESTEAD/STEEL VALLEY HIGH SCHOOL

PLAYER	POINTS	NOTES
Charlie Batch	3.0	Lengthy NFL career as both starter and backup
Joe Zuger	2.0	CFL star for more than 10 years; Arizona State University Hall of Fame
Luke Getsy	1.5	University of Akron, two-year starter; finished all-time passer in the Western Pennsylvania Interscholastic Athletic League (WPIAL)
Total:	6.5	
Average:	2.2	

6TH: BUTLER

PLAYER	POINTS	NOTES
Terry Hanratty	3.0	Solid NFL career as spot starter and backup; Notre Dame University, national champion, starting quarterback, 1966; established school records and finished tenth in Heisman voting in 1967 and third in 1968; consensus All-American
Scott Milanovich	3.0	Limited four-year NFL career; University of Maryland, three-year starter; finished all-time passer
Dale Betty	2.0	All-American Honorable Mention at the University of Maryland, 1960; still ranks high in pass percentage
Troy Nunes	1.5	Started portions of all four years at Syracuse University
Total:	9.5	
Average:	2.4	

5TH: BEAVER FALLS

PLAYER	POINTS	NOTES
Joe Namath	4.5	Pro Football Hall of Fame; University of Alabama, national champion, starting quarterback, 1964
Lou D'Achille	2.0	Solid college player at Indiana University; selected for Blue–Gray All-Star, 1952
Kevin Scanlon	2.0	Drafted by the Los Angeles Rams; University of Arkansas Hall of Fame, with an exceptional senior year
Total:	8.5	
Average:	2.8	

The website noted: "Beaver Falls only has three players, but it should be noted that Beaver Falls is a very small area with less than 10,000 residents. Three other players, Mike Weaver (Blackhawk) [and] Richard Doyle and Babe Parilli (Rochester), also were quarterbacks of some significance from near Beaver Falls."

4TH: CENTRAL CATHOLIC/OAKLAND

PLAYER	POINTS	NOTES
Dan Marino	4.5	Pro Football Hall of Fame
Marc Bulger	4.0	Underrated pro career with the St. Louis Rams; MVP, Pro Bowl, 2004; highly rated passer
Tino Sunseri	1.5	CFL quarterback, 2013–16 (had Sunseri's professional career been factored in the original scoring, he would probably rank a bit higher); University of Pittsburgh, three-year starter
Total:	10.0	
Average:	3.3	

3RD: HEMPFIELD/YOUNGWOOD SCHOOL DISTRICT AREA

PLAYER	POINTS	NOTES
George Blanda	4.0	Pro Football Hall of Fame, partly due to quarterback play, but also kicking and longevity
Bob Naponic	2.5	Single-season pro career as backup for the Houston Oilers, 1970; University of Illinois, three-year letterman, 1966–68
Tom Blanda	2.0	NFL quality, but chose military service; Second Team All-American quarterback for football power Army
Dick Vidmar	2.0	Standout at the University of Michigan; still ranks in the top 10 for many passing categories
Eddie Johns	1.0	Led the University of Miami in both passing and rushing, 1960
Matt Knizer	1.0	Had some big moments for the Detroit Lions, 1987; primarily a backup at Penn State University
Total:	12.5	
Average:	2.1	

2ND: MCKEES ROCKS

PLAYER	POINTS	NOTES
Tom Clements	3.0	Longtime CFL star; limited NFL; Notre Dame University, national champion, starting quarterback, 1973; finished fourth in Heisman voting, 1974
Chuck Fusina	3.0	Limited NFL; USFL star; Penn State University great; Maxwell Trophy winner
John Hufnagel	2.5	Played three years for the Denver Broncos; CFL player, 1976–87; Penn State University, three-year starter, including the 11–1 team in 1971 that won the Cotton Bowl; finished sixth in Heisman voting, 1972
Adam DiMichelle	1.5	Temple University, captain and team MVP
Dave Havern	1.0	University of Pittsburgh, leading passser, 1968 and 1971
Total:	11.0	
Average:	2.2	

The website indicated that "it should be noted that Frank Sinkwich, who was born in McKees Rocks, but later moved to Youngstown, Ohio, is not included here. He became a Heisman Trophy winner at the University of Georgia and a considerable NFL player before an injury shortened his career in 1947. The quantity is good here, but this group lacks a star."

1ST: DONORA/MONONGAHELA/RINGGOLD

PLAYER	POINTS	NOTES
Joe Montana	4.5	Pro Football Hall of Fame
Arnold Galiffa	3.0	Played some in NFL and CFL; College Football Hall of Fame
Scott Zolak	3.0	Eight-year NFL quarterback; significant University of Maryland quarterback, 1988–90
Lou Cecconi	2.0	Drafted by the San Francisco 49ers, but no NFL; University of Pittsburgh, 1948 and 1949, leading passer
Bernie Galiffa	1.5	West Virginia University, starting quarterback, 1970–72
Total:	14.0	
Average:	2.8	

The website indicated that this was the "best combination of quality and quantity."

RANKINGS OF "THE SIX" UPON THEIR RETIREMENTS

HERE'S A LIST of The Six and where they ranked on the all-time lists for several offensive categories at the time of their retirement. Only top-20 rankings are listed here. Notice the sheer domination in the touchdowns-thrown department—upon their retirement, all six of the featured quarterbacks from Western Pennsylvania were in the top 12 for touchdown passes, and five of them were in the top 10! Furthermore, both Unitas and Marino finished their careers as the No. 1 all-time passer for total completions, yards, and touchdown passes.

Many quarterbacks have since passed The Six in some departments due to longer seasons, different rules, and a more recent emphasis on the passing game, but within their time frame, the rankings of The Six were phenomenal and prolific. In fact, many of their rankings are still very impressive.

ALL-TIME RANKING UPON RETIREMENT

	LAST SEASON	COMPLETIONS	PASSING YARDS	TD PASSES	COMPLETION %
John Unitas	1973	1	1	1	9
George Blanda	1975	10	10	7	[20+]
Joe Namath	1977	11	12	7	[20+]
Joe Montana	1994	3	4	4	2
Jim Kelly	1996	8	10	12	5
Dan Marino	1999	1	1	1	9

SOURCES CITED

BOOKS

Berger, Phil. *More Championship Teams of the NFL.* New York: Random House, 1974.

Callahan, Tom. *Johnny U.: The Life and Times of John Unitas.* New York: Crown, 2006.

Carroll, Bob. *When the Grass Was Real: Unitas, Brown, Lombardi, Sayers, Butkus, Namath, and All the Rest.* New York: Simon & Shuster, 1993.

Conner, Floyd. *Football's Most Wanted: The Top 10 Book of the Great Game's Outrageous Characters, Fortunate Fumbles, and Other Oddities.* Lincoln, Neb.: Potomac Books, 2000.

Cook, Kevin. *The Last Headbangers: NFL Football in the Rowdy, Reckless '70s—the Era That Created Modern Sports.* New York: W. W. Norton & Company, 2012.

Delsohn, Steve. *Talking Irish: The Oral History of Notre Dame Football.* New York: Perennial/HarperCollins, 2001.

Garner, Joe. *And the Crowd Goes Wild: Relive The Most Celebrated Sporting Events Ever Broadcast.* Naperville, Ill.: Sourcebooks MediaFusion, 2002.

———. *And the Fans Roared: The Sports Broadcasts That Kept Us on the Edge of Our Seats.* Naperville, Ill.: Sourcebooks, 2000.

Grabowski, John F. *The San Francisco 49ers Trivia.* San Diego: Lucent Books, 2003.

Hersch, Hank. *Greatest Football Games of All Time.* New York: Time-Life Education, 1998.

Herskowitz, Mickey. *The Golden Age of Pro Football: A Remembrance of Pro Football in the 1950s.* New York: Macmillan, 1974.

Herzog, Brad. *The Sports 100: The One Hundred Most Important People in American Sports History.* New York: Macmillan General Reference, 1996.

Horrigan, Joe, and John Thorn, eds. *The Pro Football Hall of Fame 50th Anniversary Book: Where Greatness Lives.* New York: Grand Central Publishing, 2012.

Jenkins, Dan. *Saturday's America.* New York: Little Brown, 1970.

Kelly, Jim, with Vic Carucci. *Armed and Dangerous.* New York: Doubleday, 1992.

Kriegel, Mark. *Namath: A Biography.* New York: Viking, 2004.

Levy, Marv. *Where Else Would You Rather Be?* New York: Sports Publishing, 2012.

Maki, Allan. *Football's Greatest Stars.* Richmond Hill, Ontario: Firefly Books, 2015.

McGinn, Bob. *The Ultimate Super Bowl Book: A Complete Reference to the Stats, Stars, and Stories behind Football's Biggest Game—and Why the Best Team Won.* Minneapolis: MVP Books, 2012.

McMahon, Dave. *Miami Dolphins. Inside the NFL.* Minneapolis: ABDO Publishers, 2010.

O'Brien, Jim. *Glory Years: A Century of Excellence in Sports.* Pittsburgh: James P. O'Brien Publishing, 2000.

———. *Hometown Heroes: Profiles in Sports and Spirit.* Pittsburgh: James P. O'Brien Publishing, 1999.

———. *Pittsburgh Proud: Celebrating the City's Rich Sporting History.* Pittsburgh: James P. O'Brien Publishing, n.d.

Ogilvie, Bruce, and Thomas Tutko. *Problem Athletes and How to Handle Them.* London: Pelham Books, 1966.

Patoski, Joe Nick. *The Dallas Cowboys: The Outrageous History of the Biggest, Loudest, Most Hated, Best Loved Football Team in America.* New York: Back Bay Books, 2013.

Roberts, Randy. *Pittsburgh Sports: Stories from the Steel City.* Pittsburgh: University of Pittsburgh Press, 2000.

Schefter, Adam, ed. *The Class of Football: Words of Hard-Earned Wisdom from Legends of the Gridiron.* New York: William Morrow, 2009.

Smith, Robert. *Illustrated History of Pro Football.* New York: Madison Square Press, 1972.

Stadler, Mike. *The Psychology of Baseball: Inside the Mental Game of the Major League Player.* New York: Gotham Books, 2014.

Stewart, Wayne. *The Little Giant Book of Basketball Facts.* New York: Sterling, 2005.

———. *Stan the Man: The Life and Times of Stan Musial.* Chicago: Triumph Books, 2010.

Stowers, Carlton. *Staubach: Portrait of the Brightest Star.* Chicago: Triumph Books, 2010.

DOCUMENTARIES

Dougherty, Sean J., Stuart R. Ross, and Earl Mann. *The Greatest Moments in Western Pennsylvania Sports History.* DVD. [Pittsburgh]: Ross Sports Productions, [2005].

Lavine, Joe, and Keith Cossrow, producers. *Namath: Beaver Falls to Broadway.* On-demand video. Executive producers, Rick Bernstein and Steve Sabol. New York: HBO Sports Production, Home Box Office, Inc., 2012.

INTERVIEWS

Andabaker, Rudy. Phone interview, ca. July 2010.

Berry, Raymond. Phone interview, February 23, 2012.

Caudill, Tom. Phone interview, ca. March 2012.

Cecconi, Bimbo. Phone interview, ca. February 2012.

Cox, Fred. Phone interview, ca. February 2012.

Crawley, Carl. Phone interview, ca. July 2012.

Crummie, Chuck. Phone interview, January 25, 2012.

Ditka, Mike. Phone interview, January 24, 2012.

Emanuele, Joe. Phone interview, January 26, 2012.

Erdelyi, Rich. Phone interview, January 25, 2012.

Fabin, Stanley. Phone interview, ca. February 2012.

Ferguson, Vagas. Phone interview, ca. March 2012.

Finder, Chuck. Phone interview, January 26, 2012.

Galiffa, Bernie. Phone interview, ca. January 2012.

Gallagher, Mike. Phone interview, ca. February 2012.

Haines, Kris. Phone interview, ca. March 2012.

Havrilak, Sam. Phone interview, February 15, 2012.

Henry, Terry. Phone interview, July 15, 2014.

Higgins, Steve. Phone interview, January 15, 2012.

Houston, Jim. Phone interview, ca. June 2012.

Lucci, Mike. Phone interview, January 24, 2012.

MacAfee, Ken. Phone interview, ca. March 2012.

Marchetti, Gino. Phone interview, February 4, 2012.

Matte, Tom. Phone interview, January 22, 2012.

McGurgan, Betsy. Personal interview, December 2011.

Moore, Lenny. Phone interview, ca. January 29, 2012.

Nelson, Andy. Phone interview, ca. August 2012.

Payne, Ulice. Phone interview, ca. April 2012.

Ruey, Speer. Phone interview, ca. March 2012.

Sarkus, David. Phone interview, ca. February 2012.

Slager, Rick. Phone interview, ca. March 2012.

Smith, Chuck. Phone interview, ca. April 2012.

Stokes, Tim. Phone interview, ca. March 2012.

Thomas, Ken. Phone interview, January 15, 2012.

Unitas, Chad. Phone interview, July 15, 2014.

Unitas, Joe. Phone interview, ca. July 2014.

Unitas, Leonard. Phone interview, ca. January 2012.

Unitas, Paige. Phone interview, January 6, 2012.

Unitas, Sandy. Phone interview, ca. January 2012.

[Unitas] Green, Shirley. Phone interview, January 6, 2012.

Volk, Rick. Phone interview, January 10, 2012.

Ziemann, John. Phone interview, January 9, 2012.

Zolak, Paul. Phone interview, ca. March 2012.

Zolak, Scott. Phone interview, ca. March 2012.

MAGAZINES

Breslin, Jimmy. "For Namath, Frustration . . . and Blackberry Brandy." *Sport* (March 1977).

———. "The Town That Spawns Athletes." *The Saturday Evening Post* (October 15, 1955): 26–27.

Hano, Arnold. "How Mr. Blanda Built His Dream Season." *Sport* (March 1971).

Olderman, Murray. "Mike Ditka, Pro Football Find." *Sport* (May 1962).

Patrick, John. "Rating the Pro Quarterbacks." *Sport World* (December 1967).

Turan, Kenneth. "It's Not Whether You Win or Lose but How You Play the Game." *Inside Sports* (June 1981).

NEWSPAPER ARTICLES

Grupp, John. "Sideline Supremes." *Pittsburgh Tribune-Review.* August 27, 2006.

Summers (artist). "Six More Weeks of Winter." Editorial cartoon. *Beaver County Times.* February 4, 2014.

Wilner, Barry. "Namath Tops Hall Guest List." Associated Press. June 29, 2013.

ONLINE SOURCES

http://www.clemson.collegebuzzz.com/dwight-clark.php (accessed November 2014).

http://www.donora.fire-dept.net/1948smog.htm (accessed August 2017). Donora Fire Company, "Donora Smog of 1948," 2007.

http://www.espn.go.com/high-school/football/great-state-debate/story/_/id/7459739/five-states-stand-tall-qb-debate (accessed August 2017). Heather Dinich, "Five States Stand Tall in QB Debate," January 12, 2012.

http://www.espn.go.com/nfl/story/_/id/10549870/former-buffalo-bills-quarterback-jim-kelly-patiently-endures-cancer-loss (accessed August 2017). Rick Reilly, "The Patience of Jim," March 4, 2014.

http://www.louisville.edu/artsandsciences/about/hallofhonor/inductees/unitas.html (accessed August 2017). "Johnny Unitas (1933–2002)," n.d.

http://www.maxpreps.com/news/bWBu1OyGOkWc_2TfERc7RA/top-10-legendary-pennsylvania-quarterbacks.htm (accessed August 2017). Kevin Askeland, "Top 10 Legendary Pennsylvania Quarterbacks," n.d.

http://www.pbs.org/baseball-the-tenth-inning/world/no-one-walks-off-the-island/ (accessed August 2017). Geoffrey C. Ward and Ken Burns, "No One Walks Off the Island," n.d.

http://pittsburghquarterback.com/what-area-of-western-pa-has-produced-the-best-quarterbacks (accessed November 2014).

http://www.post-gazette.com/stories/local/obituaries/obituary-stan-musial-donora-pa-native-won-7-batting-titles-671247/ (accessed August 2017). Gene Collier, "Obituary: Stan Musial/Donora, Pa., Native won 7 Batting Titles," January 20, 2013.

http://www.post-gazette.com/stories/sports/high-school-football/mike-ditka-huddles-with-the-quips-of-his-alma-mater-310487/ (accessed August 2017). Craig Meyer, "Mike Ditka Huddles with the Quips of His Alma Mater," August 16, 2011.

https://www.pro-football-reference.com (accessed August 2017).

http://www.profootballhof.com/history/release.aspx?RELEASE_ID=744 (accessed August 2017). "He Guaranteed It: Joe Namath Made the Super Bowl Truly 'Super,'" January 1, 2005.

http://www.profootballhof.com/hof/member.aspx?player_id=154 (accessed August 2017). "Quarterback: 'Joe Cool' Joe Montana," n.d.

http://www.rankopedia.com/Greatest-Quarterback-from-Western-Pennsylvania-Ever/Step1/9247/.htm (accessed November 2014).

http://www.roman-emperors.org (accessed August 2017).

http://sportsillustrated.cnn.com/centurys_best/news/1999/08/13/flashback_montana2/ (accessed November 2014).

http://sportsillustrated.cnn.com/vault/article/magazine/MAG1026824/2/index.htm (accessed November 2014).

http://sportsillustrated.cnn.com/vault/article/magazine/MAG1125149/index.htm (accessed November 2014).

http://www.steelers.com (accessed August 2017).

INDEX